HISTORICAL TOURS
FREDERICKSBURG

HELP US KEEP THIS GUIDE UP TO DATE

We would love to hear from you concerning your experiences with this guide and how you feel it could be improved and kept up to date. Please send your comments and suggestions to:

editorial@GlobePequot.com

Thanks for your input, and happy travels!

HISTORICAL TOURS

Fredericksburg

Trace the Path of America's Heritage

RANDI MINETOR

With an introduction by James C. Bradford

Photographs by Nic Minetor

gpp®

Guilford, Connecticut

gpp

An imprint of Rowman & Littlefield

Distributed by NATIONAL BOOK NETWORK

Copyright © 2015 by Rowman & Littlefield

Maps by Trailhead Graphics, Inc. © Rowman & Littlefield
Historical interior maps courtesy of the Library of Congress.
All photographs by Nic Minetor, except for the following: Photos on pp. 1, 2, 3, 4, 5, 8, 9, 10, 11, 12, 13, 15, 16, 17, 18, 20, 25, 29 (bottom), 38, 41, 44, 50, 52, 57, 69, 80 courtesy of the Library of Congress.

All rights reserved. No part of this book may be reproduced in any form or by any electronic or mechanical means, including information storage and retrieval systems, without written permission from the publisher, except by a reviewer who may quote passages in a review.

British Library Cataloguing in Publication Information Available

Library of Congress Cataloging-in-Publication Data Available

ISBN 978-1-4930-1294-7 (pbk.)
ISBN 978-1-4930-1776-8 (e-book)

∞™ The paper used in this publication meets the minimum requirements of American National Standard for Information Sciences—Permanence of Paper for Printed Library Materials, ANSI/NISO Z39.48-1992.

> All the information in this guidebook is subject to change. We recommend that you call ahead to obtain current information before traveling. All restaurants are open daily for breakfast, lunch, and dinner, unless otherwise noted.

Contents

Introduction 1
Key Participants 10
The Days before the Battle 19
The Battlefield Tour 31
Before the Battle 33
Day 1: December 11, 1862 37
Day 2: December 12, 1862 46
Day 3: December 13, 1862 55
Beyond the Battlefield: Enriching Your Experience 89
Historic Fredericksburg: A Tourist's Guide to Exploring, Staying, and Eating 93
Glossary 105
Bibliography 107
Index 109

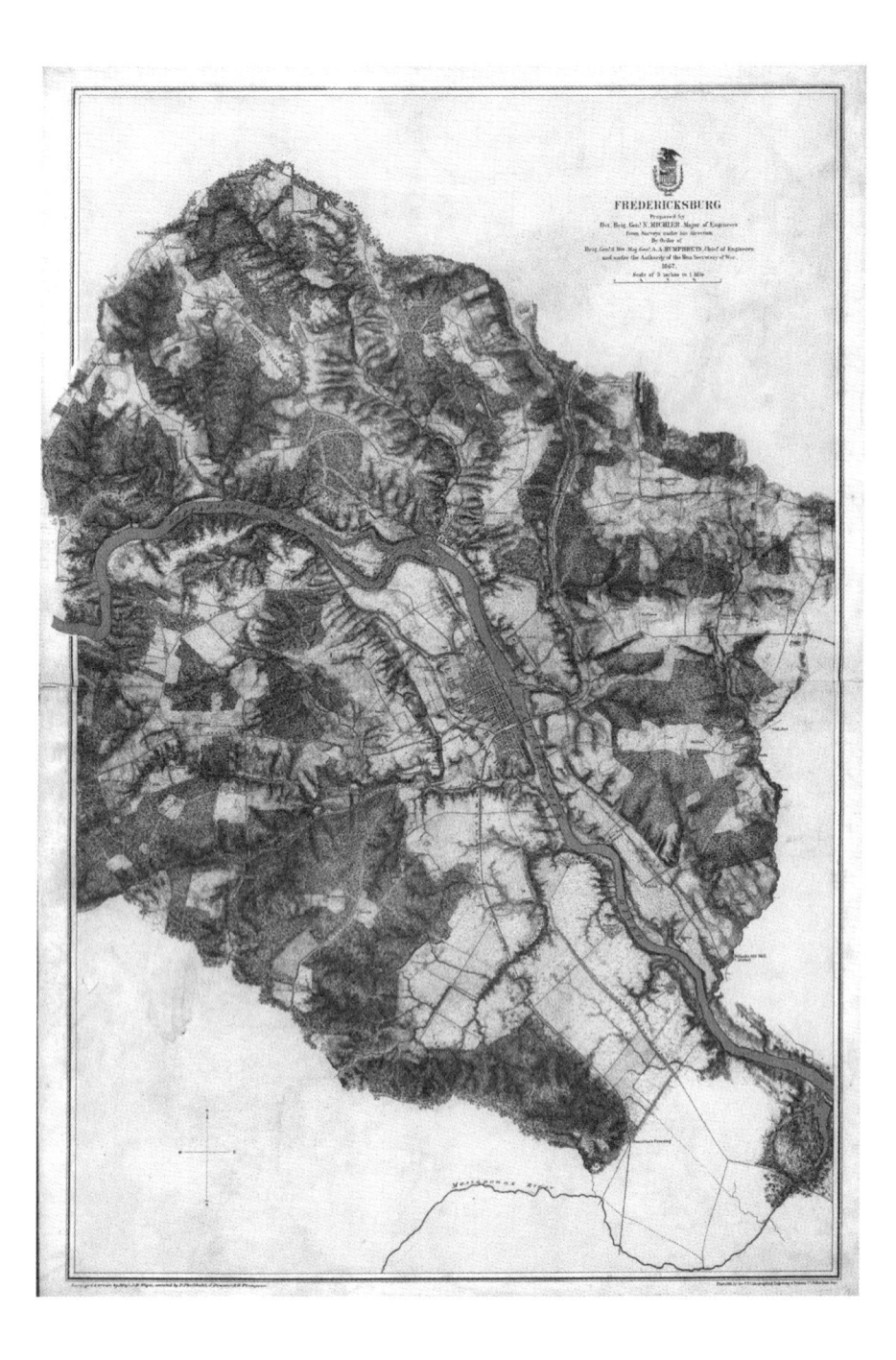

FREDERICKSBURG

Introduction
by JAMES C. BRADFORD

Fredericksburg, a town with a population of 5,000 in 1862, lies on the west bank of the Rappahannock River, roughly midway between the Federal capital at Washington and the Confederate capital at Richmond. With such a location in the vital northern Virginia theater of war, it was inevitable that the town would feel the effects of the Civil War. The battle fought at Fredericksburg on December 13, 1862 was among the one-sided victories in the Civil War and concluded the Union offensive into Virginia at the end of the second campaigning season of the Civil War.

The year 1862 had witnessed see-sawing action in a series of campaigns. Union forces took the offensive first, in March, when Major General George B. McClellan bypassed strong Confederate positions in northern Virginia by transporting his Army of the Potomac down that river to Fort Monroe, on the tip of the peninsula formed by the York and James Rivers. From there "Little Mac" advanced cautiously northwestward in the direction of the Confederate capital at Richmond. The slowness of his movements gave Confederate

Fredericksburg served as a navigation and trade hub in the 1860s.

McClellan passed through Fredericksburg in September 1862.

commander Joseph E. Johnston time to transfer much of his army from positions near Centreville to the Peninsula. Johnston was wounded during the battle at Fair Oaks, May 31–June 1, and succeeded as Confederate commander by General Robert E. Lee. His losses at Fair Oaks (also known Seven Pines) checked the Union advance and reinforced McClellan's cautiousness. Inconclusive engagements followed at Oak Grove, June 25; Mechanicsville, June 26; Gaines's Mill, June 27; Ganett's and Golding's Farm, June 27-28; Savage's Station, June 29, and White Oak Swamp, June 30, before Lee ordered a frontal assault on the Union lines at Malvern Hill, July 1. His troops suffered heavy losses, but the attack convinced the naturally timid McClellan to pull back to Harrison's Landing and remain there until mid-August, when President Abraham Lincoln ordered him to abandon the Peninsula Campaign.

Meanwhile, a second Union advance toward Richmond, this one from the north by Major General John Pope's Army of Virginia, was turned back at Cedar Mountain, near Culpepper on August 9. At the end of that month Thomas "Stonewall" Jackson turned on Pope, hoping to defeat him before McClellan's troops could arrive from the Peninsula. Elements of the two

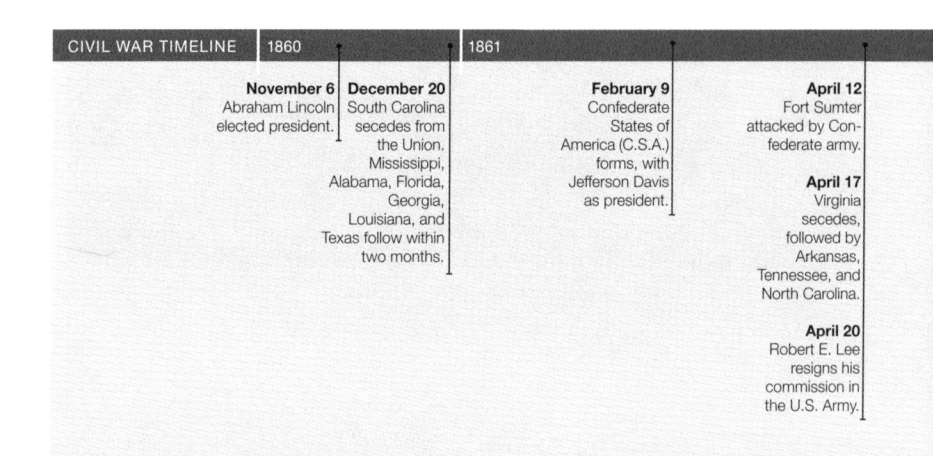

CIVIL WAR TIMELINE	1860		1861	
	November 6 Abraham Lincoln elected president.	**December 20** South Carolina secedes from the Union. Mississippi, Alabama, Florida, Georgia, Louisiana, and Texas follow within two months.	**February 9** Confederate States of America (C.S.A.) forms, with Jefferson Davis as president.	**April 12** Fort Sumter attacked by Confederate army. **April 17** Virginia secedes, followed by Arkansas, Tennessee, and North Carolina. **April 20** Robert E. Lee resigns his commission in the U.S. Army.

armies met at Brawner House, August 28. The following morning the main armies fought the Second Battle of Bull Run (which the Confederates called Second Manassas), August 29-30, which was followed by an engagement at Chantilly, September 1, and forced Pope to retreat into Washington. A day later President Lincoln relieved Pope of his command, restoring McClellan to command of all Union forces in Virginia.

The Second Battle of Bull Run resulted in a strong Confederate victory.

Emboldened by success, Lee launched an invasion of the North, one that was stopped at Sharpsburg, near Antietam Creek, in Maryland, on September 17, the single bloodiest day of battle in North American history. McClellan's Army of the Potomac effectively blocked the invasion, but his failure to pursue Lee aggressively as the Army of Northern Virginia retreated southward led Lincoln to replace McClellan as Union commander with Major General Ambrose Burnside. Between September 1861 and July 1862, Burnside had led a series of successful attacks on Confederate positions along the coast of North Carolina and the state's Outer Banks, climaxing in the capture of Roanoke Island on February 8 and New Bern on March 14. Leaving behind garrisons to prevent Confederate recapture of these important ports, Burnside returned with most of his troops to Washington. Lincoln offered Burnside

1862

July 21
First Battle of Bull Run (First Manassas)

November 1
President Lincoln appoints George B. McClellan general-in-chief of the U.S. armed forces.

January 31
Lincoln issues General War Order No. 1, calling for U.S. forces to advance by February 22.

February 6
Major General Ulysses S. Grant captures Fort Henry in Tennessee, and Fort Donelson ten days later.

April 6 and 7
Confederates surprise Grant at Shiloh; 23,000 men are killed or wounded in the fighting.

April 24
Flag Officer David Farragut leads seventeen Union ships to take New Orleans.

Major General Burnside took command of the Army of the Potomac on November 7, 1862.

command of the Army of the Potomac after McClellan's failure in the Peninsula Campaign, and a second time after Pope's defeat at Second Bull Run. Aware of his limitations, Burnside declined to accept command both times, the second time telling Lincoln that he "was not competent to command such a large army." When ordered, not asked, to assume command of the Army of the Potomac after Antietam, Burnside reluctantly accepted the position on November 7 and, at Lincoln's urging, immediately planned an offensive against Richmond. McClellan, for his part, left the army on December 11, never to return nor ever to accept his replacement as being anything but the unjust result of jealousy on the part of fellow officers, including Major General Henry W. Halleck, whom he held responsible for influencing Lincoln.

In the aftermath of Antietam Lee divided his army, sending Jackson to Winchester in the northern Shenandoah Valley to prevent any Federal incursion into that vital supply region, and Major General James Longstreet to Culpepper to protect that crossing of a north-south railroad with another running from the

1862

May 31
Battle of Seven Pines: Confederate General Joseph Johnston attacks near Richmond, checking the Union advance on the Confederate capital.

June 1
General Robert E. Lee replaces Johnston and assumes command of the Confederate army.

June 25–July 1
The Seven Days Battle near Richmond; McClellan begins withdrawal from the South.

July 11
General Henry Halleck becomes general-in-chief of the Union army.

August 29–30
Second Battle of Bull Run (Second Manassas): Major Generals James Longstreet and Stonewall Jackson and 55,000 soldiers defeat the Union's forces of 75,000 men.

September 4–9
The Confederate army invades Harper's Ferry, West Virginia.

September 17
Battle of Antietam: 26,000 men are dead or wounded by day's end.

September 18
Lee's army crosses the Potomac, withdrawing that evening to Virginia.

September 22
Lincoln issues a preliminary Emancipation Proclamation.

Shenandoah Valley to Richmond. As September turned into October and November, Lee expected both armies to abandon campaigning for the season and to enter winter quarters.

Such was not to be. When he took command of the Army of the Potomac, Burnside decided on an offensive. His first move was to reorganize the army into three "grand divisions," each composed of two corps: Major General William Franklin's division contained the I and VI Corps, Major General Edwin Sumner's division the II and IX Corps, and Major General Joseph Hooker's the III and V Corps. Burnside could hardly have selected three poorer commanders as his chief subordinates. None was known for initiative or inspiring leadership. Many of his corps commanders were better—they could hardly have been worse—but none commanded the same troops they had at Antietam.

Next came Burnside's plan for employing his army: Richmond would remain his chief target. Rather than focusing on destroying Lee's army, Burnside decided on an aggressive move to swing his army eastward around the Confederates' fortified lines, to cross the Rappahannock River at Fredericksburg.

Union troops destroyed railroad bridges to Fredericksburg when they left the town in August.

1863

November 7
Lincoln replaces McClellan with Major General Ambrose Burnside.

December 13
Burnside is roundly defeated at Fredericksburg, losing more than 12,000 men to the Confederate army's 5,300.

January 1
Lincoln issues the formal Emancipation Proclamation, freeing all slaves in Confederate territories.

January 25
Lincoln replaces Burnside with Major General Joseph Hooker.

May 1-4
Lee defeats Hooker at Chancellorsville; Stonewall Jackson is wounded and dies on May 10.

Knowing the Yankees had destroyed most bridges across the Rappanhannock, Burnside planned to rely on portable pontoon bridges for the crossing and then to move directly on Richmond before Lee could shift the Army of Northern Virginia into a position to block him. Lee was indeed caught off guard.

The plan received Lincoln's approval on November 15, and Burnside set off at once. Stealing a march on Lee, the advance elements of Burnside's 114,000-man army reached the east bank of the Rappahannock by November 17, well in advance of the time it took his opponent to move his army there. Three days later, Burnside's entire army was on the river. Rather than striking boldly across the Rappahannock, he deployed Sumner's Division on the north or upriver end of the Union line behind the village of Falmouth on the Union side of the river; Hooker's Division in the center directly opposite Fredericksburg; and Franklin's to the south on the Union left. He devoted several days to arranging more than 300 cannon in positions to support his infantry.

Some of his subordinate commanders urged Burnside to seize the opportunity to ford the Rappahannock before Lee could get his men into position, but Burnside demurred, choosing to await the arrival of the pontoons he had ordered for bridging the 400-foot-wide river. Burnside feared that subdividing his force to ford the river might subject it to piecemeal defeat as the units crossed the river. Instead he waited nearly three weeks for the pontoons and bridging equipment to arrive, a decision which gave Lee time to reach the area and deploy his 72,500-man army and 275 guns in formidable positions. When Lt. General James Longsteet's men arrived on November 21, some took up positions along a sunken road and behind a stone wall while the rest began digging in atop Marye's Heights. Soon they spread out along a line anchored on the left

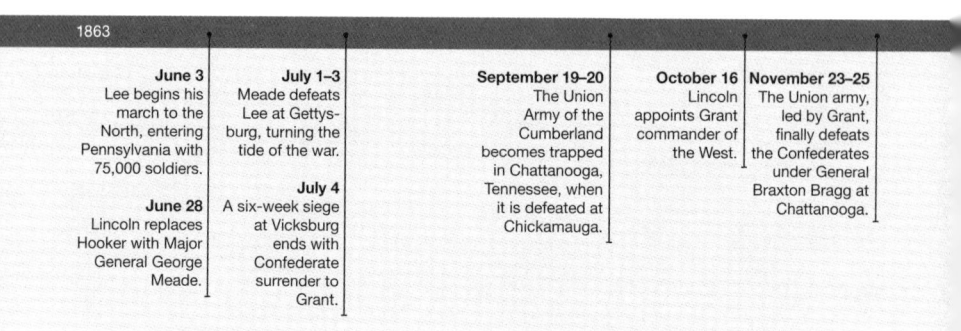

1863

June 3
Lee begins his march to the North, entering Pennsylvania with 75,000 soldiers.

June 28
Lincoln replaces Hooker with Major General George Meade.

July 1–3
Meade defeats Lee at Gettysburg, turning the tide of the war.

July 4
A six-week siege at Vicksburg ends with Confederate surrender to Grant.

September 19–20
The Union Army of the Cumberland becomes trapped in Chattanooga, Tennessee, when it is defeated at Chickamauga.

October 16
Lincoln appoints Grant commander of the West.

November 23–25
The Union army, led by Grant, finally defeats the Confederates under General Braxton Bragg at Chattanooga.

on Taylor's Hill to Hamilton's Crossing near Massaponax Creek on the left. Lt. General Jackson's men followed and deployed to Longstreet's right, downstream along Prospect Hill, with J.E.B. Stuart's cavalry covering their flank.

Meanwhile, Burnside equivocated, first considering sending one of his divisions twelve miles downriver to cross the Rappahannock at Skinker's Neck, from which it could return north and attack Lee's right, then abandoning the plan. Lincoln twice called him to Washington to discuss his plans, but Burnside appeared incapable of making a decision. He next planned a crossing to the south of Fredericksburg that would place his army between Lee's and Richmond, but at the last minute changed his mind and decided on a massive simultaneous frontal assault against the Confederates in and behind the town itself. On Tuesday, December 9, each of the Union soldiers was issued enough cooked rations to last three days and sixty rounds of ammunition. On the 10th most of Burnside's senior officers advised him that his plan for a frontal assault would be suicidal, but nothing deterred him. His mind was finally made up, and, at 5 a.m. the next morning, Burnside's engineers began lashing the pontoons together and overlaying them with timbers and earth to form three bridges. Later that day Union troops began crossing the river, but their attacks were piecemeal and delivered unevenly. The ensuing battle produced a bloodletting for the Union forces, which suffered 12,653 casualties, twice those of the Confederates, and a decisive victory for Lee's Army of Northern Virginia. On the night of December 15, the wind rose and it began to rain. Using the storm as cover, the Union troops recrossed the Rappahannock, removing their pontoon bridges behind them. The Battle of Fredericksburg was over. Informed of its outcome, Abraham Lincoln stated, "If there is a worse place than Hell, then I am in it."

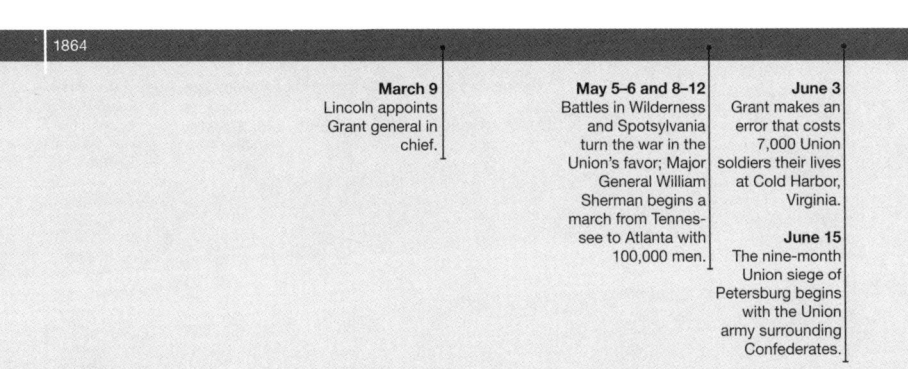

1864

March 9
Lincoln appoints Grant general in chief.

May 5–6 and 8–12
Battles in Wilderness and Spotsylvania turn the war in the Union's favor; Major General William Sherman begins a march from Tennessee to Atlanta with 100,000 men.

June 3
Grant makes an error that costs 7,000 Union soldiers their lives at Cold Harbor, Virginia.

June 15
The nine-month Union siege of Petersburg begins with the Union army surrounding Confederates.

In Stonewall Jackson's camp, men prayed for victory the night before battle.

Hundreds of Federal troops deserted in the aftermath of battle and, having lost faith in their commanders, headed for their homes. The president knew what had to be done: He accepted Burnside's resignation as commander of the Army of the Potomac, transferred the disgraced general to the West, and replaced him with Joseph Hooker. Thus, as 1862 drew to a close, Union morale reached a new low, and Confederates heartened. Observers on both sides of the Atlantic began to believe, many for the first time, that the Confederacy could prevail in the conflict and force Union recognition of its independence. Perhaps 1863 would be the year of decision.

Few Civil War battles can be envisioned as clearly as Fredericksburg over a century later. It was the only engagement fought in an urban setting. That area has been transformed by development, but the key elements of the terrain—the Rappahannock River, Marye's Heights, the ridge composed of Stansbury's Cemetery, Telegraph and Prospect Hills, and Stafford Heights—remain. An observant visitor can still trace the outlines of Jackson's trench lines on Prospect Hill, view the stone wall that sheltered Longstreet's men along the base of Marye's Heights, and view most of the battlefield from Chatham Manor.

1864

September 2 Sherman captures Atlanta.

November 8 Lincoln is reelected president.

December 5–16 55,000 Union troops defeat Major General John Hood's army at Nashville.

December 21 Sherman reaches Savannah and the sea, leaving a swath of destruction in his wake.

Efforts to preserve portions of the battlefield date to the year the war ended. In July 1865 Congress authorized establishment of a National Cemetery at Fredericksburg for the burial of Union soldiers. The site selected was on Marye's Heights and reburial of the dead began soon afterwards. The identity of more than 80 percent of the 14,000 interred is not known. At virtually the same time the Fredericksburg Ladies Memorial Association established a small cemetery for the burial of 2,640 Confederate dead; only 330 have been identified.

Brompton, the home of the Marye family during the war, still overlooks Fredericksburg National Cemetery.

The Fredericksburg National Cemetery borders the Fredericksburg Battlefield, which forms a component of the Fredericksburg and Spotsylvania National Military Park. The Fredericksburg and Spotsylvania County Battlefields Memorial National Military Park was established in 1927 and transferred to the War Department six years later. The Fredericksburg portions of the park include 1,572 acres, 84 of which are privately owned. Park headquarters are located in Chatham Manor, the Georgian brick mansion known as the Lacy House during the battle, when it served as headquarters for Union generals Sumner and Hooker.

The Fredericksburg and Spotsylvania National Military Park includes portions of two other major battlefields, Chancellorsville and the Wilderness. Together its component parts cover a total of 8,535 acres, making it the second largest military park in the United States, trailing in area only the Chickamauga and Chattanooga Military Park in Tennessee.

1865			
January 31 The Thirteenth Amendment officially abolishes slavery.	**March 25** Lee's forces in Petersburg attack Grant's army, and are defeated in four hours.	**April 2** Lee evacuates Petersburg. Richmond is evacuated. **April 9** Lee surrenders to Grant at Appomattox. **April 14** John Wilkes Booth shoots Lincoln at Ford's Theatre in Washington. Lincoln dies the next morning at 7:22 a.m. **April 18** General Johnston surrenders to Sherman in North Carolina.	**May** The C.S.A. reunites with the United States.

Key Participants

Officers of the Union

Major General Ambrose Everett Burnside
A promising officer with command potential, Burnside had already been promoted twice since the Civil War began. When President Abraham Lincoln chose him to command the Army of the Potomac on November 7, 1862, Burnside well knew the challenges ahead of him, but he obeyed his president and rose to command. At Lincoln's and Major General Henry Halleck's insistence, Burnside made aggressive plans to take Richmond in a winter campaign; we will see how these failed as part of his defeat at Fredericksburg. Burnside retained command only through January 26, 1863, when Major General Joseph Hooker was called to replace him. The rumors are true: Sideburns were named after Burnside's remarkable facial hairstyle.

Major General William B. Franklin Commander of the Left Grand Division, Franklin would take the blame from Burnside for his failure to defeat the Confederate right end at Fredericksburg, even though men under his command would make the only breakthrough of the Confederate line that occurred in battle on December 13. Franklin was appointed to the U.S. Military Academy by then-senator (later president) James Buchanan, but his military experience before the war consisted entirely of administration and construction projects as a member of the Topographical Engineers, including a period as supervisor of the Light House Board. Just before the war, Franklin had supervised construction of the U.S. Capitol Dome, and he'd just become supervising architect for the Treasury Building when the war began. As a corps commander, he fought in the Peninsula Campaign and at Antietam. When Burnside saddled him with the blame for the Union's defeat at Fredericksburg, Franklin became angry enough to play an active role in Burnside's military demise. Burnside, aware of Franklin's ire, took action against him that removed him from field duty for months.

Major General Joseph Hooker "Fighting Joe" Hooker commanded the Center Grand Division— the combined III and V Corps—at Fredericksburg, a promotion from the commission he went directly to President Lincoln to achieve shortly after the war began. A U.S. Military Academy graduate, Hooker fought in the second Seminole War and the Mexican-American War, serving with distinction until he testified against his former commanding officer, General Winfield Scott, in a court-martial case. Hooker resigned his commission under pressure in 1853 and attempted life as a farmer and land developer, finding the civilian grind dull and distasteful—but Scott had become general-in-chief of the U.S. Army, so Hooker's return to the military would take unusual ingenuity to accomplish. When the Civil War started, Hooker was in the civilian audience who came to observe the First Battle of Bull Run, after which he wrote directly to Lincoln and promoted his own ability to do a more competent job in battle. Lincoln granted him a commission as brigadier general. At Fredericksburg, Hooker was forced to lead his men in fourteen frontal assaults at Burnside's command— despite his own vociferous objections. A few weeks later, in January 1863, he replaced Burnside as commander of the Army of the Potomac.

Brigadier General Henry J. Hunt Chief of artillery for the Army of the Potomac, Hunt enjoyed a reputation as a master artillery strategist. He literally wrote the book on artillery maneuvers and tactics: *The Instructions for Field Artillery,* used by all Union artillerists throughout the war, was revered as a bible of military weapons strategy. By the time he arrived at Fredericksburg, Hunt had distinguished himself at First Manassas, Malvern Hill, South Mountain, and Antietam, the culmination of a military career that spanned the Mexican-American War—including decorations for gallantry at Contreras and Churbusco—and the 1857 Utah War against the Mormons.

Major General George G. Meade He would become the leader of the Army of the Potomac the following summer, but George Meade's courage and skill in command rose to prominence at Fredericksburg, when his division of the Union I Corps made the only breakthrough of the Confederate line in the entire battle. Meade was the son of a wealthy merchant from Philadelphia, who lost his fortune by supporting Spain in the Napoleonic Wars. Born in Cádiz, Spain, Meade graduated from West Point and became a civil engineer, then returned to the army for steady employment after he and his wife had seven children. After the Mexican-American War, Meade returned to engineering and designed Barnegat Light on Long Beach Island, Absecon Light in Atlantic City, Cape May Light in New Jersey, and Jupiter Inlet Light in Florida. The Civil War drew him back into the military.

Major General John F. Reynolds Reynolds commanded the I Corps at Fredericksburg, a part of the Left Grand Division. A U.S. Military Academy graduate, he served at Fort McHenry, St. Augustine, and Fort Moultrie before reassignment to Corpus Christi, TX, for the Mexican-American War. Reynolds' western service extended to the Rogue River Wars and the Utah War with the Mormons before he was called to serve in the Civil War. Early in the war, he had his most embarrassing moment: After functioning without sleep for days at the Battle of Gaines Mill, Reynolds became a prisoner of war when he fell asleep and did not know that his troops had left him behind. He was captured and held at Libby Prison at Richmond, and was traded back to the Union army less than two months later in exchange for other high-value prisoners. He returned to duty, continuing to serve until July 1, 1863, when he was the first officer to die at Gettysburg—a fact made even more tragic because he had become engaged to Katherine May Hewitt at the beginning of the war. Hewitt was Catholic and Reynolds was Protestant, so they kept their engagement a secret and planned to marry after the war.

Major General Edwin V. Sumner Born in 1797, Sumner chose the military in 1819 after a career as a merchant, making him the oldest field commander in the entire Civil War. He commanded the Right Grand Division at Fredericksburg, one of the three divisions in Major General Burnside's reorganization of the Army of the Potomac. Legend has it that a musket ball once bounced off of his head in battle without causing an injury—earning him the nickname "Bull Head" for the rest of the war. Sumner's military career spanned the Black Hawk War and several Indian campaigns, as well as the Mexican-American War and a term as the military governor of New Mexico, from 1851 to 1853. Sumner went on to command Fort Leavenworth in Kansas, and later, the Department of the West. So distinguished was his service that he was chosen as the senior officer to accompany President-elect Lincoln from Illinois to Washington in March 1861, when threats against the new president's life made military protection necessary. Lincoln then sent Sumner to command the Department of the Pacific in California, recalling him in November 1861 to command the II Corps of the Army of the Potomac. At Fredericksburg, Sumner's most important contribution was off the battlefield: He was instrumental in talking Burnside out of a second day of frontal assault on December 14.

Officers of the Confederacy

Brigadier General William Barksdale A former lawyer, Barksdale gave up his practice to become editor of the *Columbus Democrat,* a pro-slavery newspaper in Mississippi, and then enlisted in the Second Mississippi Infantry and served in the Mexican-American War. When he returned home, he followed in his older brother's footsteps and became a "States' Rights Democrat" in the U.S. House of Representatives, working against abolition at the federal level. The onset of the Civil War saw Barksdale rise to the leadership of a military contingent of Confederate sharpshooters known as Barksdale's Mississippi Brigade—a name they earned at the Battle of Malvern Hill, where Barksdale took command of the brigade when General

Richard Griffin was mortally wounded. Barksdale led a heroic charge against the Union, and while the assault failed, his courageous actions led to his promotion. Barksdale's Brigade was Fredericksburg's first line of defense against the Union advance across the Rappahannock on the morning of December 11, using sniper fire from hiding places in bombed-out buildings to slow the crossing.

Brigadier General Thomas R. R. Cobb Before the Civil War, Cobb served as a reporter for the Supreme Court of Georgia, a position that may have come to him when he married the daughter of one of the justices. Cobb penned a document that became famous for its support of slavery, *An Inquiry into the Law of Negro Slavery in the United States of America,* and his fervor for states' rights led him to become a delegate to Georgia's Secession Convention of 1861. On December 13, 1862, Cobb became the target of a bullet fired from the vicinity of the home on Hanover Street in which his parents were married. He bled to death from this wound in his thigh before the day was over.

Major General Thomas "Stonewall" Jackson One of only a handful of commanders whose names became synonymous with bravery and tenacity for their performance in the Civil War, Jackson led the Army of Northern Virginia's Second Corps at Fredericksburg. He earned his nickname at First Manassas in July 1861, where he and his disciplined men stopped the Union assault on Henry House Hill with a relentless attack at close range, complete with the first use of the rebel yell. After this battle, Jackson was promoted from lieutenant general to major general, and in the next year he would become Lee's most trusted officer. Jackson's ability to move his men great distances in comparatively short amounts of time—and then win battles, even with a fraction of the opposing force's men—made him the second most famous officer in the Confederacy (after Lee). Just before the Battle of Fredericksburg, two significant things would happen to Jackson: first, he received news of the birth of his daughter; and second, he received a gift from cavalry officer Major General J. E. B. Stuart, who gave Jackson the fine general's coat that became the leader's trademark.

General Robert E. Lee The venerable General Lee resigned his commission in the United States Army days after the Civil War began in 1861, and he assumed command of the Army of Northern Virginia on June 1, 1862. When he was appointed general-in-chief, newspapers criticized the choice and speculated that the mild-mannered leader would be too timid in his approach to battle with the Union army. Lee quickly turned public opinion with his highly aggressive tactics in the Seven Days Battles, forcing Union Major General George McClellan into a retreat. Public support grew for Lee as he resisted McClellan's forces at Antietam, proving his strength under pressure. When President Lincoln replaced McClellan with Major General Ambrose Burnside after Antietam, Lee soon saw that his army had the upper hand. He took full advantage of his enemy's weaknesses at Fredericksburg, bringing home a handy victory with a far lower casualty rate than his opponent.

Major General James Longstreet Another of Lee's most trusted corps commanders, Longstreet commanded the Army's First Corps with such aplomb that he is still hailed by historians as one of the best commanders—if not the best commander—in the entire war. His comprehension of strong defensive tactics gave the Confederate army a competitive advantage in battles including the Second Battle of Bull Run and Antietam. At Fredericksburg, Longstreet proved his worth once again by arriving early and ordering the construction of trenches and earthworks, to block the enemy's fire and shelter the defensive line. Protected in dugouts behind taller breastworks, Longstreet's men avoided much of the Union fire throughout the December 13 battle—and as a result, only 500 Confederate men fell, compared with 10,000 Union soldiers, during the assault on Marye's Heights.

Brigadier General William N. Pendleton The chief of artillery for the Army of Northern Virginia, Pendleton attended West Point at the same time as Lee, along with soon-to-be Confederacy president Jefferson Davis. Pendleton served in the military after his years at the academy, then left the army and became an Episcopalian priest, teaching at an Episcopal boys' high school in Delaware. He had become a church rector when the war began, but he answered the call to arms and became captain of the Virginia Artillery—maintaining his religious spirit by naming his four guns Matthew, Mark, Luke, and John. Promoted to artillery general for the Army of Northern Virginia in July 1861, Pendleton is remembered most for a misstep after the Battle of Shepherdstown, in which he lost some of his big guns to Union forces while he commanded the rearguard infantry overnight along the Potomac River. His performance at Fredericksburg, however exemplary, would do little to restore his tarnished reputation. After the war, Pendleton returned to the church in Lexington, Virginia, where Lee became part of his congregation.

Major General J. E. B. Stuart The flamboyant Major General Stuart, always an expert horseman, led the cavalry of the Army of Northern Virginia to a victory at First Battle of Bull Run, the first of many major accomplishments that include his legendary ride all the way around Union forces at Richmond without being detected. Never one to sacrifice style for stealth, Stuart wore a plumed hat and bright cloak into battle—and lost them famously in a Federal raid. However, Stuart quickly retaliated the following day, surprising the Union at Catlett's Station and capturing U.S. Major General John Pope's full uniform at his headquarters office. At Fredericksburg, he and his cavalry protected the Confederate army's right flank at Hamilton's Crossing.

The Days before the Battle

As the Virginia sun descended into the late fall chill on December 10, 1862, Major General Ambrose Burnside stood on the northern bank of the Rappahannock River and reflected on a strategy that had gone terribly wrong.

Responding to pressure from President Abraham Lincoln and General-in-Chief Henry Halleck, Burnside had planned an aggressive offensive against the Confederate Army in central Virginia. He knew that Major General George McClellan, the personal friend whom he had succeeded as leader of the Army of the Potomac a month before, had been replaced because he had not performed to Lincoln's expectations. McClellan was not aggressive enough for the president, who wanted a decisive end to a war that had cost tens of thousands of lives in its first year alone—and would surely lead to much more bloodshed before it was over.

Just two days after he took command on November 10, 1862, Burnside sent a plan of decisive action to Lincoln and Halleck for their approval. Burnside originally planned to make Confederate General Robert E. Lee believe that he'd concentrated the Union troops near Warrenton, Virginia, in preparation for an attack on one of the area's courthouses or on nearby Gordonsville.

From the northern bank near Chatham, Burnside saw Fredericksburg through the mist and fog.

The Union gathered in Falmouth, upriver from Fredericksburg.

With Lee preoccupied near Warrenton, Burnside would then move his army forty miles southeast to Fredericksburg at a rapid pace, placing Lee at a defensive disadvantage. This would also allow Burnside to avoid an encounter with Stonewall Jackson's troops in the Shenandoah Valley, a battle that could deplete the Union army's resources without resulting in tangible gains in ground or supply lines.

Once across the river from Fredericksburg, Burnside's forces would construct pontoon bridges and cross into town within a day, giving the Confederate army no time to put a defensive line in place before the Union took the town and secured this strategic location. With a stronghold between the Confederate States of America's capital in Richmond and the United States' capital in Washington, DC, the Army of the Potomac would have the power to block supplies to Richmond, a major advantage that could turn the tide of the war.

The plan received quick approval, but both Lincoln and Halleck emphasized the need for speed: If the plan was to work, it would have to be completed before the Confederate army had time see Burnside's intention and construct defensive lines against it. The commander-in-chief and his general urged Burnside to make haste.

Taking the president's words to heart, the newly appointed, 38-year-old general selected Falmouth, Virginia, as his supply base, and began amassing provisions there in anticipation of the move. He ordered the 120,000 troops camped around Warrenton to quick-march to a position just across the river from Fredericksburg, where he was told that the pontoon bridge equipment and parts he needed would be waiting for him on November 17.

In just three days, three Union "grand divisions"—each with two corps and its own executive staff, a structure that Burnside believed would strengthen the army by streamlining operations—arrived on the banks of the Rappahannock, ready to build bridges and cross the river. They arrived on schedule on November 17 . . . but the pontoon bridges did not.

The Rappahannock was too deep and wide to cross without bridges.

Despite assurances Burnside had received from the War Department that the bridge supplies would meet him on the riverbank when he arrived, the pontoon bridge materials were actually fifty miles behind the army at the Potomac River. Through a convoluted set of message delays, the necessary pontoon boats were en route to Washington instead of Fredericksburg. McClellan had ordered the pontoons to Washington on November 6, just before he was relieved of command. The pontoons reached Washington on November 14, and did not leave the capital until November 19—so all that awaited Burnside on his arrival near Fredericksburg was a telegraph message from Brigadier General Daniel P. Woodbury that the engineers and supplies "had not been able to get off."

With only about a thousand Confederate soldiers assembled on the other side of the river, the Union could have taken Fredericksburg with a minimum of resistance if their means of crossing the river had arrived as planned. Instead, Burnside and his men camped near the Richmond, Fredericksburg & Potomac (RF&P) Railroad in Falmouth and waited, watching as their advantage dribbled away.

Major General Edwin V. Sumner, the oldest and most seasoned military

The Union set up its big guns on Stafford Heights.

officer on the field, was first to arrive in nearby Falmouth with the Right Grand Division on November 17. He saw his advantage over the sparse ranks of the opposing army, and ordered his division to march to the river and attempt an immediate crossing. The 42nd Mississippi infantry had tracked Sumner's advance, however, and gathered in ambush at the Falmouth ford, ready to push the Union troops back. In a hail of artillery fire from each side, the Union scattered the Confederate battery in fifteen minutes. "They drove every man on the other side from the guns," Sumner later reported. "They ran off and left four guns in the field." Still eager to cross the river while Fredericksburg was so lightly defended, Sumner reported the Confederate skirmish to Burnside, who advised against a crossing—even at the passable ford Sumner found upriver. Instead, the Union army assembled its substantial artillery on Stafford Heights overlooking the Rappahannock, putting Fredericksburg and its western high ground well within range of the Union's biggest guns.

Over the next several days, as rains swelled the river and Burnside and his officers examined and rejected one alternate plan after another, it became clear that the Union army had no choice but to wait for the pontoons. Burnside wrote to the War Department on November 19, " . . . examination of the fords here today demonstrated that the Infantry and Artillery cannot pass . . . I cannot make the promise of probable success with the faith that I did when I supposed all parts of the plan would be carried out."

Surrender or Be Shelled

Knowing that Lee and his army had to be on their way to Fredericksburg, Burnside attempted to take the city by negotiation before the Confederate troops arrived. On November 21, Burnside sent a missive through Provost Marshal Marsena Patrick to the mayor of Fredericksburg, ordering the government officials to surrender the town by 5:00 p.m., or face bombardment from the Union's artillery on the Stafford Heights at 9:00 the next morning. The time lag between surrender and shelling was actually a merciful one, intended to give civilians time to evacuate the city before the artillery fire began. The message to the mayor, however, was intercepted by the Confederate troops, who insisted that it be sent through military channels—so instead of arriving on the mayor's desk, the letter found its way to Lee's tent, where he was meeting with generals James Longstreet and Lafayette McLaws.

The response that finally arrived hours later on Burnside's side of the river informed the general that the Confederates were already entrenched on the high ground above Fredericksburg, and that there would be no surrender. The opportunity for an easy seizure of Fredericksburg had passed; Burnside was now faced with the probability of a full-scale confrontation with the Army of Northern Virginia.

What Fredericksburg's Mayor Montgomery Slaughter bargained for, however, was that both sides would hold their fire until the women and children had left the town. After considerable negotiation that also involved two Confederate officers (Brigadier General Joseph E. Kershaw and Colonel Elbert Bland), Provost Patrick agreed that the Federal army would allow the evacuation and would not fire until fired upon by the Confederates.

With the handwriting so clearly on the wall, civilians packed up to leave town as fast as they could, with women, children, and the elderly fleeing on foot, on horseback, and by train—even in the cattle cars—toward farms, churches, and the homes of friends well outside of town. Of the more than 5,000 residents, only a handful remained to protect their homes—and a fair

"Almost the entire population, without a murmur, abandoned their homes. History presents no instance of a people exhibiting a purer and more unselfish patriotism or a higher spirit of fortitude and courage than was evinced by the citizens of Fredericksburg. They cheerfully incurred great hardships and privations, and surrendered their homes and property to destruction rather than yield them into the hands of the enemies of their country."
—**General Robert E. Lee, in his official report on the Battle of Fredericksburg**

Women and children evacuated these homes on Caroline Street and many more throughout the town.

number of the townspeople's more than 1,200 slaves found their way across the river to the protection of the Union army, beginning new lives in freedom.

The Pontoons Arrive

On November 25, the pontoons Burnside had ordered to meet him at Fredericksburg eight days earlier finally came through. As the general knew from the moment he arrived, the eight-day delay was a disaster. Not only did it hinder Burnside's occupation of Fredericksburg and rob him of his advantage, but it also allowed Lee to amass his troops, swelling his ranks to match Burnside's. Even Major General Stonewall Jackson, whose corps was stationed some 200 miles south, had enough time to reach Fredericksburg and form the right flank of the Confederate line.

Yet Washington continued to heap pressure on Burnside to act. General-in-Chief Halleck adamantly maintained that the Army of the Potomac should attack now, even if there was no possibility of success. President Lincoln, however, wanted a less risky crossing into Fredericksburg that could potentially take the town without driving the Confederates back down the road

The Union attempted a crossing at Skinker's Neck on December 5.

to Richmond, a route that would allow the Confederates to gain supplies, reinforcements, and ammunition.

Burnside spent two weeks planning his crossing, with his engineers searching under cover of night to find a spot with stable banks that would support the weight of thousands of men, horses, and artillery. Finally they chose Skinker's Neck, a bend fourteen miles down the river with appropriately solid ground, which appeared to be beyond the reach of the Confederate guard. Burnside enlisted the assistance of the U.S. Navy to send a flotilla of gunboats to cover the crossing. As the boats made their way up the Rappahannock in the dark, shots rang out from the bluffs over the river—the Confederate army knew they were coming. The ships exchanged fire with the men on land, and finally turned back downriver, leaving Burnside without a defense for the Skinker's Neck crossing.

When Burnside began his crossing at Skinker's Neck on December 5, rain changing to snow turned the troops' march into a sluggish ordeal—and with the previous day's exchange of fire with the navy ships, the Confederates guessed the Union's intentions and formed across the river, ready to intercept and drive back the Federal army. Drive them back they did: Burnside canceled the crossing and the Army of the Potomac made their way back to camp the following day, more discouraged than ever.

While the Union delayed their crossing, the Confederates built earthworks on the high ground.

Burnside's eventual defeat was nearly assured, and barely a moment's fighting had taken place. He knew the coming winter would close Virginia roads. The Union general was running out of time.

Lee's Mighty Defensive Line

Burnside had not guessed, when he began the quick march from Warrenton to Fredericksburg on November 17, that General Lee already had an inkling of his plans. Days before the Union march began, Lee sent his most dependable cavalry officer, Major General J. E. B. Stuart, "to ascertain more fully the movements of the enemy." Stuart reached Warrenton on horseback to find that the last of Burnside's troops were on the march. "It was clear that the whole Federal Army, under Major General Burnside, was moving toward Fredericksburg," Lee later wrote in his report.

In Fredericksburg, only Colonel William Ball and his 42nd Mississippians were encamped in and around the town. They alone held the riverfront while the Union's Grand Right Division under Sumner attempted its first attack on November 17, holding their position there for five days without reinforcement.

The women of Fredericksburg, leaving their homes after nightfall, brought baskets of food and drink to the exhausted men as they stood guard on the edge of the river.

At first, Lee assumed that Burnside's army would cross the river into Fredericksburg immediately on arrival. Knowing that he could not move quickly enough to stop him, Lee first ordered Major General James Longstreet to move two of his divisions to Fredericksburg, while the rest of his corps would block the road to Richmond. Meanwhile, he sent word to Major General Thomas "Stonewall" Jackson to come in from the Shenandoah Valley and head for Fredericksburg—but the distance would mean that Jackson would not arrive for more than a week. If Burnside attacked immediately, Fredericksburg would be lost—so Lee focused his efforts on the aftermath of the Union occupation of Fredericksburg, closing the road to the Confederate capital.

When Longstreet's First Corps arrived in Fredericksburg on November 19, they were surprised to discover that the Union troops were essentially stranded on the other side of the river without the equipment they needed to cross. Longstreet quietly occupied the high ground behind the town, with his troops lining the hills from the banks of the Rappahannock on Fredericksburg's left, all the way to Massaponax Creek to the right. Concealing his arrival in the woods above the town, Longstreet's divisions went undetected

Longstreet concealed his forces on the high ground, out of sight of the Union troops.

by the Federal forces. By the end of the day on November 23, five Confederate divisions had arrived, but they left Colonel Ball's 42nd Mississippians on the riverbank with no reinforcements, so the Union would not know that thousands of Confederate soldiers were now in place on the high ground.

Jackson's Second Corps began to arrive on December 1, marching 175 miles in twelve days. They formed a long extension of Longstreet's line, expanding the defensive forces all the way to Hamilton's Crossing, while Lee deployed troops that stretched his line even further, all the way to Port Royal and the Rapidan River to the south. In addition, Lee placed a battery about four miles downriver, to fire on any gunboats the Union might attempt to send up the river toward Fredericksburg. While Lee exercised this caution because he could not be sure where Burnside would attempt his attack, his action placed a fair number of his men at least a day's distance away, where they could not assist in an attack on the town.

Most important, Lee's army held the high ground, with 20,000 men of First Corps on the hills behind the town—including Marye's Heights (more on this pivotal position later).

While waiting for Burnside to make his move, Lee's army spent their time removing trees that blocked the view from Telegraph Hill, Howison Hill, and Marye's Heights, digging trenches and building earthworks on the crests of the hills above the town in places most advantageous for artillery positions.

Burnside Plans His Attack

"I think now that the enemy will be more surprised by a crossing immediately in our front than in any other part of the river," Burnside wrote to Lincoln after the failure of the attempted crossing at Skinker's Neck.

It wasn't what anyone wanted—a crossing directly into the Confederate line's center behind the town, where the enemy could hide inside civilian homes and public buildings and counter their crossing with deadly fire. Lincoln had advised against it, Burnside's officers—especially Sumner—were vocal and forthright in their criticism of the plan. Yet with the element of surprise long squandered and a well-entrenched adversary across the river, Burnside could not see any other options. He would strike at the heart of the Confederate army's position.

Burnside explained the plan to his generals in a war council on December 9. He had decided to build bridges at three points along two miles of the river: two opposite the city, and one a mile downstream.

Because Burnside held the Stafford Heights

From Ferry Farm to City Dock, Burnside's troops would strike at the heart of the Confederate line.

and placed his artillery there, he convinced himself it would be virtually impossible for Lee's army to attempt any kind of resistance to a Union river crossing without taking very heavy losses. He knew that the bulk of Jackson's forces were miles away, so the Union would only face about half of Lee's combined troops once they crossed the river. Not knowing the exact size of the Confederate army assembled on the hills above him, Burnside believed—and rightly so—that his 120,000 troops were a far greater force than Lee's entrenched defensive force. Such an attack had the potential to succeed, he told his officers.

Burnside's commanding officers, however, doubted that this plan would work, discussing the "rashness of the undertaking" among themselves. Word came back to Burnside that his generals had criticized the plan to one another, and he called a second meeting to chastise them all for their disloyalty. By the end of the day on December 10, the officers ceased their outward expressions of doubt, and began taking the necessary steps to execute the plan.

On the night of December 10, the Union camped on the Rappahannock in anticipation of the next day's events.

Pontoon Bridges

When the Union army left Fredericksburg in August 1862 after a lengthy occupation, the troops destroyed the existing bridges over the Rappahannock to make it more difficult for the Confederate army to use this pivotal position as a northern crossing. This was sound military strategy, but it made a return to Fredericksburg particularly tricky when the Army of the Potomac arrived in November.

Major General Burnside planned to bring more than 30,000 Union soldiers across such bridges on the Rappahannock River. These vast numbers of men, with their accompanying artillery and horses, could not cross the rain-swollen, rushing river on boats (which were not available in any case) or thrash their way across through the deep water.

With no bridges in place, the Union army would have to resort to temporary bridges built on pontoons—boats with flat bottoms, which were used to support a structure on water.

To assemble pontoon bridges, engineers took pontoons into the river, and connected the boats together with long side rails, called bulks. Wooden boards were placed across the bulks as bridge flooring. Engineers staked the bridge to the shore on either end, and then dropped anchor to brace the boat against the current.

Normally, engineers could lay a pontoon bridge in two or three hours, but under enemy fire it could take all day, and the dangerous task could result in considerable loss of life. Such was the challenge presented to the Union engineers on December 11, 1862, when they began the process of assembling pontoon bridges across the Rappahannock.

You can see a scale model of a pontoon bridge section behind Chatham Manor, at the overlook point behind the house. From here, you can see Fredericksburg across the Rappahannock and the high ground on which the Confederate Army of the Potomac waited for Union action.

This sample segment of a pontoon bridge is behind Chatham Manor.

The Battlefield Tour

Before you begin your walking or driving tour of Historic Fredericksburg and the battlefield, make a stop at the **Fredericksburg and Spotsylvania National Military Park Visitor Center** at 1013 Lafayette Boulevard. The 22-minute video presentation has been condensed from a longer program, *Fredericksburg: A Documentary Film,* which you can purchase in the park's bookstore (in a separate building behind the visitor center). Take the time to view this well-produced shorter program while you're in the visitor center, to understand the dynamics of troop maneuvers, weather, hills, and water that came together to favor the Confederate army and force the Union to fail on this ground. Civil War reenactors and narration by James Earl Jones help bring the story to life in this dramatic film.

The visitor center offers a small museum with many artifacts found on the battlefield, as well as uniforms and soldiers' personal items provided by descendants of those who served here. You'll find knowledgeable national park rangers and historians here, as well as helpful volunteers who can direct you to points of interest throughout the park, including the three major battles that took place here in the years after Fredericksburg: the battles of Spotsylvania Courthouse, the Wilderness, and Chancellorsville.

Stop at the National Park visitor center to see the video on the battle.

The Sunken Road and Fredericksburg National Cemetery are just outside of the visitor center. You will visit both of these sites as part of the tour, at stops 6 and 12.

Battlefield Etiquette: Respect Your National Military Park

Follow these basic rules during your visit to the Fredericksburg battlefield:

- **Park only in designated areas.** Don't pull off the road onto grass or ground. Preservation efforts are underway throughout the park, including along the sides of roadways and on fields and grassy areas.

- **Park on the right-hand side of the road only.** If all of the official parking spaces are taken at your tour stop, you are welcome to park on the road. Parking on the right side only will ensure a smooth flow of traffic along the tour route.

- **Remember that you are touring hallowed ground.** Enjoy your visit, but please refrain from climbing on cannons, monuments, or fences. Treat the park and its grounds with respect for the lives lost here, and for the magnitude of the events that took place in these farmers' peaceful fields, orchards, and woods.

Before the Battle

Tour Stop 1: Chatham Manor

The Union Commanders Lay Their Plans

During the Union's first occupation of Fredericksburg in spring and summer 1862, commanding officers used Chatham Manor—owned by the Lacy family, who were staunch supporters of the Confederacy—as their headquarters and central meeting location. Here Generals Burnside, Sumner, Franklin, and Hooker met in the days before the Battle of Fredericksburg and began to determine the best course of action, discuss all possible dangers, and make the decision at last to cross the Rappahannock River on December 11.

J. Horace Lacy had left Chatham earlier in the war to serve as a staff officer in the Confederate army. As the Union advanced on Fredericksburg in

Chatham became Sumner's headquarters during the Battle of Fredericksburg.

Chatham's main rooms still reveal some of the manor's former grandeur.

spring 1862, Betty Lacy packed up her belongings and her children and evacuated their home, moving to the family's second home at Elwood (west of Fredericksburg on Virginia Highway 3, near Grant's Headquarters on the Wilderness Battlefield).

Chatham's grandeur and its strategically advantageous position on the Stafford Heights, overlooking Fredericksburg, made it a fitting place for President Lincoln to meet with his commanders and Secretary of the Treasury Salmon P. Chase in May 1862, and for Major General Irvin McDowell to choose it as his headquarters during the spring Union occupation. When the Union returned to this position in November 1862, General Sumner quickly selected Chatham as his headquarters before and during the battle, as the Union erected its artillery on the heights and staged a massive bombardment of Fredericksburg on December 11.

During this second period as a center of Union activity, however, Chatham's elegance and richness fell into a precipitous decline. Originally a plantation with more than one hundred slaves, Chatham's fortunes changed as it was pressed into service as a field hospital during the Battle of Fredericksburg, and even became a stable for the Federal officers' horses. As the struggle for the Sunken Road and Marye's Heights raged across the river, thousands of Union soldiers made their way to Chatham for medical care, while thousands more could not travel so far and died on the field. Even those who managed to walk or be carried here often met a dismal fate: One hundred thirty of these soldiers did not survive, and were buried in the front yard of the manor house.

Of the many gruesome stories about this field hospital, one stands out for the mental image it can still evoke: Two huge catalpa trees stand behind the house, their twisted branches and contorted trunks serving as a striking demonstration of old growth. These two trees were already large in the winter of 1862, when hundreds of wounded men lay inside in critical condition. While surgeons worked feverishly to beat the spread of gangrene and infection by severing shrapnel-shattered limbs that could not be salvaged, surgeons' assistants carried these arms and legs to these trees, and piled them here between the spreading trunks. No evidence of this bloody process is visible today, but it's altogether too easy to visualize.

In the days following the battle, as doctors did their best to treat the sick and injured, two famous figures in American history were among those caring for the wounded: Clara Barton, founder of the American Red Cross and a passionate crusader for proper medicine in the field of battle; and Walt Whitman, the poet who gave us *Leaves of Grass* and many other remarkable works, who came to Chatham when he discovered that his brother, George, was listed among the wounded at Fredericksburg. George had only a minor facial wound and was not treated at Chatham, but when Whitman saw the horror men suffered in the crowded, unsanitary field hospital, he stayed to serve as a nurse and assistant, dressing wounds and helping the wounded men write letters home.

After you tour the house, walk around the back of the property to enjoy a panoramic view of the town. From here, the overlook of Fredericksburg is the best in the area, with remarkable similarities to

Surgeons' assistants used this window to discard soldiers' severed limbs beside the catalpa trees.

"The house is quite crowded, everything impromptu, no system, all bad enough, but I have no doubt the best that can be done; all the wounds pretty bad, some frightful, the men in their old clothes, unclean and bloody. Some of the wounded are rebel officers, prisoners. One, a Mississippian—a captain—hit badly in the leg, I talked with him some time; he asked for papers, which I gave him. (I saw him three months afterward in Washington, with leg amputated, doing well.)"
—**Walt Whitman, December 21, 1862**

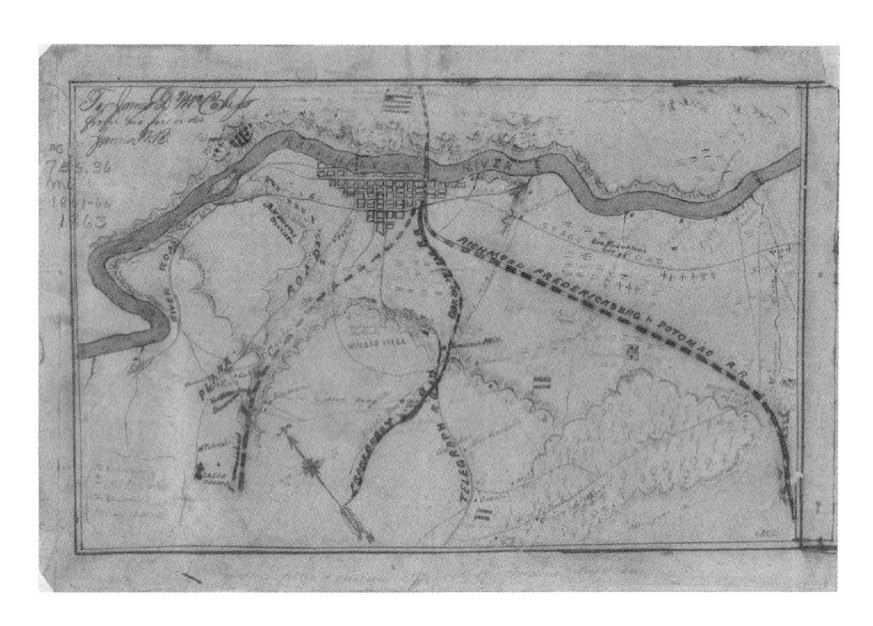

Fredericksburg was an important hub for the Richmond, Fredericksburg and Potomac Railroad, and Virginia roads, all of which met within this fairly small town.

the sights the men in hospital might have seen in 1862. Left to right, the steeples you see here of St. George's Episcopal Church, City Hall (its cupola was a surveillance point for each army), and Fredericksburg Baptist Church all rose above the town during the war.

As you leave Chatham, follow the road around Highway 3, and turn right to cross the bridge across the river and back into Fredericksburg. Turn left on Sophia Street to reach the Upper Pontoon Crossing. Park in one of the spots on the street, or use the nearby parking garage if you plan to walk around town from here.

Day 1: December 11, 1862

Tour Stop 2: Upper Pontoon Crossing (North End of Sophia Street)

The Most Dangerous Option

In the compendium of battle options available to generals on the field of war, building bridges and crossing a 400-foot expanse of an open river in full view of the enemy was one of the most dangerous choices a commander could make. With no cover and a job to do that occupies both hands—leaving no option for self-defense—the engineers on the water knew that they served as easy targets for enemy sharpshooters, and that death or serious injury might be only a few moments away.

Find the Upper Pontoon Crossing on the north end of Sophia Street.

This was the fate the New York Engineers faced in the chilly predawn fog on December 11, as they began laying their pontoons at about 3:00 a.m. They began with the Upper Crossing here at Steamboat Landing, at the end of Sophia Street, working to construct two bridges while their comrades in arms began a bridge at what is now City Dock, and two more worked at the mouth of Deep Run, farther down the river.

As the sky began to lighten, shots rang out from the Fredericksburg riverfront. Sharpshooters from Barksdale's Mississippi Brigade (which totaled 16,000 men), hidden in homes and behind fences, opened fire on the New Yorkers in an attempt to delay the bridge construction and keep the Federals back. The effort was successful: The Union men tried nine times to continue their work, but had to retreat under heavy fire. They took many

The New York Engineers could not build bridges while under fire from Barksdale's Brigade.

casualties, losing skilled engineers to a constant barrage of rifle shot.

Burnside and his officers had predicted this response from the Confederates across the water. The general ordered his artillery chief, Brigadier General Henry Hunt, to open fire on the city of Fredericksburg from Stafford Heights, where 150 of the Union's big guns were aimed at the city. Hunt began his barrage at about noon on December 11, with destructive results: Houses and businesses crashed to the ground and burned. Cannon fire shattered wooden walls and left craters in brick and marble structures, and chimneys toppled under the blasts.

After eight hours of constant bombardment, with more than 9,000 projectiles hitting the city at the rate of one hundred or more per minute and wreaking destruction on Fredericksburg's buildings and inhabitants, Burnside and Hunt believed that the barrage must have wiped out the Confederate line hidden in the houses. Certain that his men were now safe from snipers, Burnside sent the

Union engineers out on the water to build their pontoon bridges.

Almost immediately, shots rang out again from the Fredericksburg side! The Confederate sharpshooters hid in cellars along Sophia Street when the bombardment began, and managed to escape the blasts. More Union engineers went down in the frigid river waters with wounds from Confederate bullets.

Now Burnside called for volunteers to take the pontoon boats and cross the river. At about 2:30 p.m., brave men from the 7th Michigan and the 19th Massachusetts answered the call, rowing themselves across the river's 400-foot expanse while others in their boats fended off Confederate fire and returned some of their own. In short order, the Michigan and Massachusetts men established a bridgehead on the southern side of the river, taking more casualties from Barksdale's sharpshooters, but making enough headway to allow the completion of the bridge.

In short order, the 20th Massachusetts came across the bridge and made landfall in the town of Fredericksburg, rushing up the streets to engage in close combat with Barksdale's sharpshooters. After weeks of military standoff, the Battle of Fredericksburg had begun.

To continue: Walk up Hawke Street (behind you on Sophia Street). Stop at the corner of Caroline and Hawke. If you're driving, go north on Sophia Street one block to Pitt Street. Turn left on Pitt and drive two blocks to Princess Anne Street. This is one-way; turn left. Continue down Princess Anne Street to Lewis Street; turn left. Stop at the Central Rappahannock Regional Library, at 1201 Caroline Street.

Holes in brick and stone walls still remain today where bullets raked houses as the Union artillery bombarded Fredericksburg.

The post at Fredericksburg Cemetery still bears the scars of the Union cannonball.

Tour Stop 3: The Street Fight/ Central Rappahannock Regional Library

Thousands of Men in Hand-to-Hand Combat

Barksdale's men had been ordered to retreat if attacked, but they chose to stay and fight—and the battle entered the streets of beleaguered Fredericksburg, one of the few times throughout the war in which men actually fought on the streets of any town.

The fighting spread through Hawke and Caroline Streets, down Pitt Street, up the street from where you're standing at Market House and Market Square (now the Fredericksburg Museum), and finally climaxed in the area around what is now the Central Rappahannock Regional Library.

At Market Square, Barksdale kept men in reserve, sending some down the road to the town wharf—now the City Dock—to defend the riverbank where Union soldiers had constructed another pontoon bridge. This swelled the fighting even further. The 20th Massachusetts continued to advance in column up Caroline Street, losing ninety-seven men in the tightly concentrated battle. Men of the 7th Michigan took cover in an alley on the left side of Hawke Street—probably the same alley that's there today—while the 19th Massachusetts retreated to the right, back toward Pitt Street and the river, to defend the waterfront and keep the way clear for more Union soldiers to come across the bridge.

Fighting continued for ten hours up Hawke Street to Caroline, and up and down Caroline Street. Barksdale's men refused to retreat, buying

Barksdale kept some men in reserve here at Market Square (now a museum).

Soldiers fought their way up Hawke, Pitt, and Caroline Streets.

time for General Lee to get his troops into position on the ridgeline, preparing for the battle that would surely follow the next day.

When the fighting reached this area around the current library site, the charge lost momentum at last, beginning to dissipate as dusk settled in the late afternoon. With darkness upon them, Barksdale's Mississippians finally withdrew, leaving the 19th Massachusetts in possession of a row of buildings at the corner of Hawke and Caroline, and the first pontoon bridge intact and ready for the Union's crossing into Fredericksburg. In the December darkness, the Union bridge builders finally could finish the other four pontoon bridges. At last, Burnside's men entered Fredericksburg.

Continue to walk down Caroline Street, past the railroad bridge and down to Rocky Lane. Turn left on Rocky Lane and walk one block to the City Dock. If you're driving from the library, turn north on Caroline Street, and drive one block to Fauquier Street. Turn left on Fauquier and drive one block to Princess Anne Street; turn left. Drive down Princess Anne to Princess Elizabeth Street, and turn left. Princess Elizabeth ends at Sophia Street; turn right on Sophia and proceed to the City Dock. Park along Sophia Street.

"Gen. Burnside's army has made a decisive and victorious movement. The city of Fredericksburg is now occupied by his forces after a terrible bombardment, which lasted nearly all day yesterday, and resulted in the partial destruction of the city by the heavy fire of our artillery."
—***The Valley Spirit*, December 12, 1862**

Tour Stop 4: City Dock

The Union Army Makes the Crossing

Across the river from here, you can see the small farm and orchard that once served as the boyhood home of America's first president, George Washington. Ferry Farm, so named because the Fredericksburg ferry crossed the Rappahannock at this point several times daily in the 1700s, includes the orchard where Washington may have once chopped down a cherry tree, then admitted to his father that he had done so . . . if the legend is true. Visitors are welcome to walk the orchard and believe what they like about the esteemed Washington and his childhood.

On December 11, 1862, the Union built its second set of pontoon bridges here and fought its way into Fredericksburg, its engineers receiving much-needed defensive cover from the 89th New York.

Walk down the Rocky Lane from Caroline Street to reach City Dock.

Just as their counterparts had done at the Upper Pontoon Crossing, the New York division crossed from Ferry Farm to City Dock in pontoon boats, helping to push back the Confederates as Union engineers worked to build the bridges. The New Yorkers became part of the street fighting with Barksdale's Brigade until the Confederates' retreat at dusk.

Across the three bridges constructed here, the two to the north and one more to the south at Deep Run, the Union troops finally began their crossing during the night of December 11 and all day on December 12. Cold, dense fog covered the majority of the Union troops' movements as they poured into Fredericksburg, one column after another crossing the river with little resistance from the Confederate army. It took half the night and all of the following day for the Union men to walk the swaying pontoon bridges and march into town.

The New York Division crossed from Ferry Farm in pontoon boats to fend off enemy fire.

It took all day and night for Union troops to cross the river.

The Union army had made history, managing to complete the first bridge construction under enemy fire ever accomplished by the United States. The achievement came at a price, however: Forty-nine of the New York Engineers were killed or wounded in the fighting, and as many as 300 of the 3,000 infantrymen who had defended the bridge construction and fought in town were now casualties of the battle.

In the meantime, as the battle waged along the river, the Confederates had time to reinforce their defensive line along the Sunken Road, and Jackson moved his men closer to Fredericksburg, placing his own headquarters at Hamilton's Crossing, about seven miles down the road and at the end of the Confederates' right flank. Barksdale's stubborn defense in town bought Lee the time he needed to create an impenetrable line along the high ground, ready in expectation of a major battle on December 12.

When you're ready, turn around and walk back

up Rocky Lane and turn left on Caroline Street. Look for four Greek revival townhouses on Caroline Street, numbered 132 through 138. These buildings (which are not open to the public) stood here during the battle, and 132 and 134 took considerable damage—long since repaired—during the long bombardment on December 11. Soldiers occupied 136 and 138 Caroline Street at various times over the next two-and-a-half years, and artillery fragments still remain in the walls at 136. During reconstruction, a Union soldier's signature was found on an original wall in 138.

On Caroline Street, walk north to Hanover Street, and turn left. If you're driving, go north on Caroline to Charlotte Street, and turn left. Continue up Charlotte to Jackson Street. Turn right on Jackson, which ends at Hanover Street. Turn right on Hanover. Proceed slowly to note the addresses of the houses (none of which are open to the public).

These row houses on Caroline Street took major damage during the Union bombardment.

Day 2: December 12, 1862

Tour Stop 5: Hanover Street

The Sacking of Fredericksburg

Beyond occasional bombardments from Stafford Heights—many in answer to Confederate fire—Burnside did not attack the Confederates on December 12.

Burnside and his officers spent most of their time at the headquarters the general had occupied at Phillips House, a home that once stood off the current White Oak Road on Stafford Heights, observing the troop movements as they crossed into town over the pontoon bridges.

How long does it take to move tens of thousands of troops over five unsteady pontoon bridges, each only wide enough to handle single-file traffic? One division after another made the chaotic crossing on the night of December 11 and during daylight on December 12; most were finally over the bridges by late afternoon. Once the fog burned off, temperatures rose to a comfortable fifty-six degrees, encouraging a more leisurely crossing even as artillery fire ripped through the sky over soldiers' heads. The Union and Confederate gunners continued to send barrages in each other's directions, some of these raining down on Union divisions standing on the wharves in Fredericksburg, hastening them to seek cover in town.

Once over the river, some divisions of the Union army received assignments from their commanders through Major General Franklin, moving to form the right flank of the Union line. Sumner, meanwhile, constructed the left flank. When all of the generals met with Burnside toward evening at the luxurious Mannsfield mansion—which would be destroyed in the battle to come—they convinced their commander that an attack before dawn the next day would be the most advantageous course, and that Franklin's division should lead the attack at Prospect Hill, where the Confederate line seemed thinnest. Burnside left the meeting to return to his headquarters at Phillips House, but did not arrive for several hours. His whereabouts remain a mystery, and while historians believe he lost his way in the dark, the hours that passed between his departure from Mannsfield and his arrival at Phillips House delayed the necessary written orders he needed to distribute to his generals before the next day's attack.

Meanwhile, Union soldiers in town, under orders from their officers, went looking in the bombed out, fragmented houses for food, tobacco, and medical supplies to restock the field hospital. Soon this petty theft degenerated into vandalism and destruction as men looted the town, breaking down doors and taking or smashing everything they found inside townspeople's homes. Soldiers cleaned their guns with ladies' silk underwear, pulled mattresses out in the street to avoid sleeping in mud, and made coffee in silver pitchers lifted from kitchens and parlors. Some claim that soldiers only looted the homes that were unoccupied, so as not to harass residents who remained, but tenets of the soldiers' accustomed code of ethics nevertheless fell by the wayside as the men plundered a wholesale liquor establishment, filling their canteens with whiskey and forgetting their purpose in coming to Fredericksburg.

"There was considerable looting. I placed a provost-guard at the bridges, with orders that nobody should go back with plunder. An enormous pile of booty was collected there by evening. But there came a time when we were too busy to guard it, and I suppose it was finally carried off by another set of spoilers."
—**Major General Darius Couch, Union army**

While many of the homes that stood here during the war were damaged beyond repair, the homes at 801 Hanover and 408 Hanover were standing at the battle's end. Neither of these is open to the public, but you can enjoy these examples of period architecture as you walk up Hanover Road. In particular, 408 Hanover retains a cannonball in its upstairs wall. The two flanking houses, 407 and 409, were built in 1844 and also withstood the battle.

The impressive late Georgian style house that stands at an angle to Hanover Road is Federal Hill, built by Virginia governor Robert Brooke in 1792. This house became a field hospital for the Union army during several campaigns that raged through Fredericksburg. It is said that the shot that would kill Major General Thomas R. R. Cobb on December 13, 1862, was fired from here—which is ironic, because he visited this house as a child. While this is private property, you can see from the sidewalk that there are indentations still in the chimney from the Union bombardment on December 11.

Walk down Hanover Street to Princess Anne Street, and turn left. Continue two blocks to the Fredericksburg Museum (two buildings), on the corner of Princess Anne and William Streets. If you're driving, turn left on Caroline Street from Hanover, and drive three blocks to Amelia Street. Turn left on Amelia, and drive one block to Princess Anne Street. Turn left, and look for a parking place; the museum will be on your left in one block.

The house at 801 Hanover Street withstood the Union barrage and the looting on December 11 and 12.

Federal Hill stood here at 504 Hanover Street during the battle.

Tour Stop 6: Fredericksburg Museum

Preparation and Confusion before Battle

The museum in Market Square offers excellent background on the looting of Fredericksburg on December 12, as well as additional perspective on Fredericksburg's role in the war. The main museum (on Princess Anne Street) provides the larger story of Fredericksburg and its role in four wars: the Revolutionary War, Civil War, and World Wars I and II.

Learn more about the events of December 12 by visiting the Fredericksburg Museum.

Here on the spot where Barksdale's Brigade regrouped on December 11 before continuing to fight in the streets, let's pause to consider the Confederate army's actions as looting raged in the town of Fredericksburg.

Stonewall Jackson and his men arrived in the morning and joined the lines on the heights behind the town, moving under cover of fog—just as the Union men did as they crossed the pontoon bridges. As he directed Jackson and his men into position at the Confederates' right flank, Longstreet placed big guns at Taylor's Hill, Marye's Heights, Howison Hill, and Telegraph Hill (later renamed Lee's Hill), from which Lee observed most of the battle.

At the end of the line below Marye's Heights, Brigadier General Thomas R. R. Cobb's men from Georgia held a section of Telegraph Road, the main road to Richmond—known here as the Sunken Road. Wagons traversed this highway for many decades, wearing it into a deep rut several feet below the surrounding surface and accompanying stone retaining wall. Longstreet immediately recognized the road's usefulness as an excellent defensive trench. Cobb's men were positioned along the wall.

Jackson's men were on Prospect Hill, just 65 feet above the surrounding land. He strengthened his position by lining his divisions up one behind the other. Seven miles wide

Cobb's men held a section of this road, and were well protected behind the stone wall.

and nearly a mile thick, his defensive lines waited and watched the open expanse below them for Union troop movements.

By the end of the day on December 12, with no aggressive action taken save the sacking of Fredericksburg's most genteel homes, it became clear that the Union would not attack that day but that some kind of offensive must be planned for December 13. The Confederate line settled down to wait for Burnside's next move.

Burnside had fully expected Lee to surrender once the Army of the Potomac occupied the town, but even though Burnside's forces outnumbered Lee's by a third (120,000 Union troops vs. Lee's 78,000), Lee held the high ground and maintained the competitive advantage. To Burnside's men, it appeared that the general had no next move planned. "After getting in the face of the enemy, his intentions seemed to be continually changing," wrote II Corps commander Major General Darius Couch.

Seeing how well entrenched Lee's forces were to the west and south, Burnside knew that an attack on Lee's flanks would be lost before it began. He could not turn Lee's flanks without recrossing the river and attacking from Stafford County. After making such a forceful commitment to cross at Fredericksburg, this was an unacceptable option.

Burnside's commanders presented him with a plan at a 5:00 p.m. meeting at Mannsfield: Attack Lee's right flank at Hamilton's Crossing with the full force of Franklin's Grand Left Division, while simultaneously attacking the left flank with Sumner's Grand Right Division. At the time, Burnside agreed

"It is the night before a battle . . . The camp fires blaze with unwanted brightness, the sentry's tread is still but quick—the acres of little shelter tents are dark and still as death, no wonder for us as I gazed sorrowfully upon them. I thought I could almost hear the slow flap of the grim messenger's wings, as one by one he sought and selected his victims for the morning."
—**Clara Barton, in a letter to her cousin on the night of December 12, 1862**

Before the battle, Mannsfield—the home of a farmer named Bernard—served as a field headquarters for the Union army.

and told them he'd issue his orders in three hours, but ten hours later, at 3:00 a.m., John Reynolds announced he was going to bed—without any orders issued by Burnside.

Where was the general? Once Burnside arrived at Phillips House after a considerable delay, he continued to try to reason out a plan throughout the night. Thousands of troops could not pass through the marshy ground near Massaponax Creek, so an attack on that end of the line was out. An attack on Lee's left would require an open crossing of the Fredericksburg Canal, making Burnside's men sitting ducks for Lee's forces on the high ground above. The only option, Burnside believed, was to attack Marye's Heights, which were closest to town and would require the least time out in the open before the Union troops would run headlong into Lee's line.

To this plan, Burnside added an additional option: attack simultaneously at Prospect Hill, as Franklin had suggested earlier, where the height was less lofty than at the line's other end. This was the area held by Stonewall Jackson.

Burnside finally wrote his orders at around 6:00 a.m. on December 13, and sent them to his commanders via a messenger who arrived at Mannsfield at 7:30 a.m. He told Franklin—who had sat up all night waiting for these orders, expecting to attack at dawn—to "keep your whole command in position for a rapid movement down the old Richmond Road," and "send one division at least" to attack and "seize—if possible" Hamilton's Crossing, "taking care to keep it well supported and its line of retreat open." Franklin, an engineer by trade, took the orders' literal meaning in the context of war. He determined from the ambiguous wording that Burnside did not want him to attack in force, but instead to simply send a single division. Unfortunately, Burnside had meant exactly the opposite: Historians believe he intended for Franklin's attack to be the stronger of the two, concentrating full force on Prospect Hill. The vague language and hastily written orders would have significant consequences for the Union army.

To Sumner, Burnside sent the orders to attack from the upper part of town, keeping the Confederates' left flank occupied at Marye's Heights and the Sunken Road so that Franklin could take Prospect Hill. Sumner disseminated these orders to his commanders, and Major General Darius Couch began forming his divisions into columns that

> "Heavy fog and mist hid the whole plain between the heights and the Rappahannock, but under cover of that fog and within easy cannon-shot lay Burnside's army. Along the heights, to the right and left of where I was standing, extending a length of nearly five miles, lay Lee's army."
>
> **—Lieutenant William Owen, Confederate Washington Artillery**

Burnside chose to attack Marye's Heights, which lay beyond the Sunken Road.

would follow one after the other into the fray at the Sunken Road, at the base of Marye's Heights.

At the end of the day, the Army of the Potomac had a plan and the commanders had their orders, for better or worse.

When you have visited the museum, return to your vehicle to proceed to Fredericksburg and Spotsylvania County National Battlefield Park. From the museum at the corner of Princess Anne and William Streets, drive south on Princess Anne to Lafayette Boulevard. Turn right on Lafayette and continue to the battlefield's visitor center at 1013 Lafayette Boulevard. There is parking behind the center.

The Sunken Road walking trail begins just west of the parking area. Walk to the beginning of the trail and turn right onto the Sunken Road. The road is closed to vehicular traffic here.

Day 3: December 13, 1862

Tour Stop 7: The Sunken Road

The Union Marches into Disaster

On the foggy morning of December 13, Lee breakfasted quietly at Braehead House at the base of Telegraph Hill, and returned to the top of the hill before the fighting began. Burnside had just sent his orders to his commanders at about 6:00 a.m., and he remained at Phillips House as his generals received the orders and shared them with their corps commanders. The fog persisted through sunrise and into late morning, but the first Union division began its advance toward the Confederate army at 8:30 a.m., under cover of the morning mist that signaled another unseasonably warm day.

Confederate marksmen lined up behind the stone wall and awaited Sumner's attack.

Major General George Meade and a mere 3,800 men were the first to move out, heading for the Confederate right flank and a weak spot in the defensive line. We'll learn more about their breakthrough at Tour Stop 10.

Here at the Sunken Road, Sumner had orders to wait to attack Marye's Heights until he had received word of Franklin's success on the Confederate right flank. That word never came—Franklin had sent just one division into battle, as he believed the orders told him to do. By late morning, Burnside sent orders to Sumner to commence his attack.

To begin their offensive, the first of eighteen Grand Right Division brigades in the 30,000-man column had to cross the Fredericksburg Canal (now Kenmore Road), a five-foot-deep, fifteen-foot-wide ditch full of icy water, with just three rickety bridges to facilitate the crossing. With no cover, the Union soldiers were pelted with Confederate fire as they crossed. Once they forded the canal, they knocked down fences around the town's fairgrounds and used the grounds' buildings as cover. This would be their last opportunity to remain out of sight, however: After the fairgrounds, they were in the open for 300 to 400 yards, making them easy targets for the artillery above on Marye's Heights.

The first goal was the Sunken Road, on which you are standing. The road here is no longer sunken, but in the 1860s this was the most-used wagon and horse road for travel through central Virginia—and so much travel wore a deep trench that defined the route. Local residents called it the Country Road, and then Telegraph Road, but pass-

Confederate soldiers under Cobb and Kershaw hold the stone wall.

ing armies during the Civil War renamed it as they did so many landmarks—by the way it looked. As you follow along the length of the wall that stands here today, you can see the results of two reconstruction projects that took place in the 1930s and in 2004, replacing the wall with two distinctly different masonry styles.

Well-armed Confederate infantry lined up behind the original wall along the road, using it as effective cover from enemy gunfire and shelling. No sooner did the Union column begin to enter the open expanse than Confederate artillery at Marye's Heights began their bombardment. Men fell in their tracks and remained where they fell. More men passed them and continued to move forward, and the Confederates continued to fire on them until they fell as well. As each brigade made what progress they could and fell back, the next one would begin its advance.

From the top of Marye's Heights, Longstreet observed the battle below.

Meanwhile, the stone wall protected Longstreet's marksmen. Using a firing technique called "depressing the muzzle," the Confederates could shoot over their fellow soldiers' heads to reach the Union troops—so they didn't need to expose themselves to enemy fire as they took down the approaching soldiers. Only a fraction of the Confederate infantry at the stone wall were affected by Union fire. From his position on Telegraph Hill, Lee expressed concern to Longstreet about his men at the Sunken Road, but Longstreet replied, "Give me plenty of ammunition, and I will kill them all before they reach my line." Longstreet was true to his word: No Union soldier ever reached the Sunken Road. The closest brigade came only within forty yards of the stone wall.

At the end of the day, all eighteen Union brigades attempted the crossing to Marye's Heights. More than 7,500 Union men were killed, wounded, or missing, and many of these men lay on the field of battle, wounded beyond the ability to move, while the survivors had no choice but to leave them as they were or be killed or wounded as well by enemy gunfire from the heights.

The Union advance had failed miserably, with no ground gained. The only consolation came from the fact that the Confederacy gained no ground either; in essence, the casualties produced by the Battle of Fredericksburg had not resulted in progress on either side of the war. The Union was beaten, but the victorious Confederates had not advanced their position.

After the war, the Sunken Road became a city street, with houses along its length. The National Park Service began reclaiming this land as part of the historic battlefield in the 1930s, removing houses and assigning the Civilian Conservation Corps to reconstruct the first section of the stone wall.

At various stops as you walk the Sunken Road Trail, you will learn about some of the individuals whose deeds merit recognition at this national park site:

Confederate Brigadier General Thomas R. R. Cobb marker: Cobb, a constitutional lawyer before the war, fell on the spot where this marker stands. Cobb's mother's childhood home was Federal Hill (on Fredericksburg's Hanover Street). An artillery shell fired from Federal Hill hit the Stephens House, across the road from this spot, and the flying shrapnel hit Cobb's femoral artery (in his leg). Cobb bled to death on the field. Some accounts say that the wound was actually from a Confederate rifle—we will never know for cer-

This stone marks the spot where Brigadier General Cobb received a mortal wound.

tain, although deaths from "friendly fire" were not uncommon during the Civil War or in virtually any other military conflict.

Stephens House foundation: Martha Stephens ran a grocery and bar in her home here on Telegraph Road. Throughout the battle, as Confederate soldiers used the building as cover and shot at Union troops through its windows, she refused evacuation and tended to the Confederate wounded at tremendous personal risk, using strips of her own clothing to bind their wounds. She continued to live here until 1888, and she is buried to the left of the outline of the house.

Martha Stephens's home stood here, in the midst of the battle.

Innis House: An interior wall of this modest, carefully restored country home still bears the scars of bullets that penetrated it (easily seen through the window). The day before the battle, Union soldiers had looted this home, leaving little of use to the residents when they returned.

Richard Kirkland monument: He's known as the Angel of Marye's Heights by both sides of the conflict, and for good reason: This nineteen-year-old Confederate sergeant of the Second South Carolina Volunteers risked his life to bring water to the wounded Union men left on the field December 14 and 15. Positioned behind the stone wall where he had shot to kill approaching Union troops the day before, Kirkland listened to the piteous cries from the seriously wounded soldiers left on the battlefield on December 14, and decided that he could not stand allowing human beings to suffer so terribly. With the permission of his senior officer, Brigadier General Joseph Kershaw, Kirkland gathered up all the canteens he could, filled them at a nearby well and carried them out on the field of

You can see the bullet holes in the Innis House wall through the front window.

The merciful work of Richard Kirkland is remembered with this monument.

death for the Union soldiers. The Federals fired on him at first, but once they realized that his intentions were merciful, they stopped shooting and began to cheer him. Kirkland died at the Battle of Chickamauga the following year, but his work is remembered with this monument.

Ebert House: This foundation marks the location of a German entrepreneur's former home. Ebert owned a grocery store in town, and he and his family evacuated when told to do so before the battle. They came home after the Union's retreat to find dead bodies strewn across their lawn and their house a mesh of bullet holes. The home was repaired and stood here until the 1950s.

Brompton: This was the home of lawyer and businessman John Marye (pronounced Mar-ee), who owned the land that included Marye's Heights. During the battle, the house became the headquarters of Washington Artillery of New

Could a Full Frontal Assault Work?

Knowing the result of the Union's march on the Confederate-held high ground at Fredericksburg—and the outcome of similar assaults at Gettysburg and Cold Harbor—it's easy to determine that the commanding officers in all of these cases made absurd decisions in attempting a full frontal assault on well-defended ground.

At one time, however, the frontal assault had been a viable offensive strategy, because the weapons in the artillery's arsenal did not have the remarkable range and force of a new big gun used in the Civil War: the rifled-bore cannon.

Before this new weapon came into common usage, artillery units used smoothbore guns, which fired at a low velocity and had a range of a few hundred yards at best. They lacked accuracy, because the need to load these guns in great haste on the field of battle required that the ball be fairly loose in the barrel—so it actually bounced around in the barrel, making its final direction uncertain. Smoothbore guns allowed the approaching army to gain much more ground before succumbing to cannon fire, strengthening their advance and their chances of winning the battle.

Rifled-bore cannons have grooves inside the barrel, which eliminate the bouncing and actually cause the ball to spin as it leaves the gun. This improves the ball's stability, which in turn increases its accuracy and range. A ball fired from a rifled cannon could hit a target nearly two miles away.

The Union had these long-range guns and used them when they bombarded the town of Fredericksburg on December 11—so it was no mystery that these guns were powerful. The Confederates placed rifled-bore guns along the heights at the tops of Telegraph Hill, Howison Hill, Marye's Heights, and Prospect Hill. Had the Confederates still used smoothbore cannons—many were in use throughout the war—the Union might have had a chance of succeeding with a full-frontal assault. With rifled-bore cannons, however, the Confederates picked off Union soldiers while they were in open fields, even from more than a mile away.

Smoothbore cannon

Rifled-bore cannon

Orleans commander Colonel James B. Walton. Later, it was used as a Union field hospital during the 1864 Overland Campaign. Today, it's the private residence of the president of the University of Mary Washington, and is not open to the public.

From the Sunken Road, walk or drive south on Lafayette Boulevard to Lee Drive. Turn onto Lee Drive (left). This is the National Park Service road through Fredericksburg Battlefield, which follows the Confederate high ground from its northern flank at Sunken Road/Marye's Heights to its southern terminus at Prospect Hill. The route is seven miles long, and a walking trail follows the road from end to end. If you walk this route, you will need to walk seven miles back as well, for a total of fourteen miles.

Park at Lee's Hill (the park's tour stop 3), and walk up the quarter-mile paved trail from the parking area to the top of the hill. The steady incline has several switchbacks, making it a moderate climb.

Tour Stop 8: Lee's Hill

Holding the High Ground

(Note: This is the park's tour stop 3.)

From this hill—known as Telegraph Hill at the time of the battle—Lee watched the Union attacks on his troops at Sunken Road. Lee spent the entire period of the battle on this hill, first awaiting the attack and then observing its progress.

Lee's Hill is in the center of the Confederate line. To the left, the line extends to Marye's Heights and the Sunken Road. To the right, it continues to Prospect Hill. Directly below, the third Union crossing of the Rappahannock took place to the right, between Lee's Hill and Prospect Hill.

The hill was heavily wooded when troops arrived here, but Confederate pioneers spent days cutting down trees to clear the view for the

Lee observed the Battle of Fredericksburg from this hill.

general. Pioneers were special detachments from each regiment—they took the place of engineers in Lee's army (the Union armies traveled with engineers to supervise such activities). These pioneers also dug the trenches and built breastworks all along the seven-mile Confederate line. By the time the Union struck on December 13, the Confederates had made their position impenetrable.

From here, Lee could survey the entire area of battle. He watched as Burnside sent six Union divisions across an open field against Longstreet's men at Marye's Heights and Jackson's four-deep divisions at Prospect Hill. From here, artillery officer Brigadier General William Pendleton fired on the Union and kept the enemy advance at bay.

Had Burnside been able to cross the river and take Fredericksburg on his original timetable, this heavy artillery would not have been in position to hinder his advance. The three-week delay, however, allowed Lee's artillery division to transport

From here, Lee could see either end of the Confederate line.

"It is well that war is so terrible. We should grow too fond of it."
—**General Robert E. Lee on Lee's Hill, observing his troops driving the Union back from the hill into Deep Run on December 13, 1862**

all of these cannons up this hill to the top. With so many big guns firing from above, the Union attackers could not even approach the hill, and no Union soldiers had the slightest chance of charging to the summit. Confederate artillery hit them while they were still in the fields below, turning the farmland at the base of the hill into a killing field.

While Lee was in little danger from Union artillery at this height, he did narrowly escape serious injury or death twice during the battle. First, a 36-pounder Parrott rifle—much like the cannon you see here at this viewpoint—exploded and scattered metal chunks at great velocity all over the area. It was a simple stroke of luck that the flying debris did not hit Lee or Longstreet. Later in the morning, a Union artillery shell fired from Stafford Heights made landfall here, digging itself into the Confederate earthworks dangerously close to Lee. Once again, luck won out—the shell did not explode.

A cannon exploded on this hill, but Lee and Longstreet were unhurt.

The Gallant John Pelham and a Single Cannon

Among the tens of thousands of men on the field of battle, some stories of individual heroism stand out. One such story is now told in the parking lot of a pharmacy on Virginia Highways 2 and 17.

Confederate Major John Pelham commanded the horse artillery for Major General J. E. B. Stuart. A man of some military accomplishment, he saw an opportunity and persuaded Stuart to allow him to take advantage of it: Pelham would bring a single cannon to this spot at what is now called Pelham's Corner, where he could fire down the length of the Union battle line just 400 yards away. The action would startle the Union men, distract them from their advance, and buy some time for the heavy artillery and defensive line on the hillside behind him.

Stuart reluctantly agreed, urging Pelham to take cover when the position became too hazardous. Using only a small artillery crew to keep the risk to others as distant as possible, Pelham positioned his gun and began firing, drawing Union fire toward him and away from the hillside. He continued firing one round after another, confusing and exasperating the Union gunners—and even when Stuart ordered Pelham to stop for the artillery officer's own safety, he continued to fire until he ran out of ammunition.

Pelham's deeds delayed the Union advance by an hour, exhausting the Federal soldiers and drawing fire away from his generals' position on the high ground. Today you can see his exact position at the end of the Union line by visiting the marker at 10744 Tidewater Trail, at the corner of Benchmark Road.

Tour Stop 9: Howison Hill

Outmanned, Outgunned . . . and Victorious

(Note: This is the park's tour stop 4.)

Howison Hill represents another strong artillery position for the Confederate army. With several weeks to get their guns into position, the Confederate artillery had time to move a 30-pound siege gun here, a cannon that could fire a 30-pound shell nearly two miles. Siege guns are not normally found on battlefields—generally they are too large and heavy to move easily for battle, so they are used in permanent installations like forts. The big gun's extraordinary force provided a competitive advantage for the Confederates on Howison Hill.

Directly across the river on Stafford Heights, Burnside had lined up his own artillery: 381 guns,

Confederate artillery at Howison Hill included a siege gun.

Breastworks built by Confederate soldiers made this position stronger.

including some with as much firepower as this huge cannon. The Confederates had 304 guns, significantly fewer than the Union's artillery—but the Army of Northern Virginia had the advantage of position, with guns stationed at regular intervals along the Fredericksburg heights.

As the Union soldiers began to cross the open expanse between the town and the high ground, the Confederates rained cannon fire down on them from this position and three hundred others on the high ground. As a result, the Confederate army emerged at the end of the day on December 13 with 5,300 casualties from the three-day battle, compared with 12,600 Union men who were dead, wounded, or missing at the close of the campaign.

The two big cannons you see here are similar to those used in the battle. The larger, 30-pounder Parrott gun is the cannon on the left.

As you walk or drive along the road from here, you can see the earthworks constructed by Confederate pioneers in the weeks before and after the battle. The Army of Northern Virginia continued to fortify this position once the December 1862 battle had ended, with the understanding that the Union would be back to try to take Fredericksburg again. So strong was this visible line of fortifications that Major General Joseph Hooker, returning as predicted to this area during the Chancellorsville campaign, decided to skip another assault on Fredericksburg's high ground in favor of the less fortified town to the west.

Continue down Lee Drive and across Highway 638 to the Union Breakthrough (the park's tour stop 5).

The picnic area that you see between Howison Hill and the next tour stop is where Major General George Pickett's 9,000 men held the line for the Confederacy, spread across this area between Howison and Prospect Hills. Pickett's division was not attacked, and remained in reserve in battle after battle, until they finally engaged in combat at the famous Pickett's Charge in Gettysburg on July 3, 1863.

The road through here winds through a deciduous oak, ash, and holly forest, and crosses Deep Run, a small but important waterway through the battlefield. As the day's fighting wore on, the Union VI Corps, under the leadership of Brevet Major General William Farrar "Baldy" Smith, came up Deep Run in an attempt to break through the Confederate line. The Confederate infantry was stationed here at the bottom of the hills, while southern artillery lined up one cannon after another at the top of each hill. The Union army made some progress here, advancing as far as the railroad that

The Union VI Corps attempted a break through the Confederate line at Deep Run.

you see in the valley below—but once across the railroad, they engaged Lieutenant Colonel Evander Law's Brigade, who pushed the Union troops back across the tracks.

As you cross Highway 638, you'll reach Lansdowne Valley, where Longstreet's right flank joined with Jackson's left, unifying the Confederate line.

Tour Stop 10: Bernard's Cabins

A Plantation Takes a Beating

Take the one-mile (out and back) trail through the woods here to the site of cabins that housed the slaves of Mannsfield, a plantation that stood here at the time of the Battle of Fredericksburg. The path crosses the woods to the meadow, and follows the mowed path to a spot with two interpretive signs posted by the National Park Service. The trail can be muddy in wet weather, so be sure to wear proper footwear for this walk.

One of the area's most prosperous plantations, Mannsfield was founded in 1766 by Arthur Bernard and, at the time, was one of the largest mansions in Virginia. The mid-Georgian-style home fell prey to shelling in 1863, but during the Battle of Fredericksburg, the mansion served as headquarters for Union generals Franklin, Reynolds, and Smith.

Originally, an assortment of "dependencies" stood here: Three two-room cabins housed as many as thirty-five slaves, while some outbuildings and a stone-lined well provided necessities for the owner and his family. The cabins did not survive the battle.

The Confederates made this high spot above Bernard's fields an artillery position, placing nine cannons here to defeat the Union's attack on Jackson's front. At noon on December 13, Union infantry attempted to break through the line at a point ahead and to the right of where you're standing. Confederate Captain Greenlee Davidson ordered his men to fire on the approaching troops, and his artillerymen sent double cannon rounds of canister shot into the Union infantry at a deadly range of 300 yards. "The Yankees broke . . . you never saw such a stampede in your life," Davidson wrote later.

Despite this "stampede," however, the Union continued to hammer on the Confederate line here, engaging in one spirited duel after another. "By day's end, Confederate artillery was battered, Bernard's Cabins were in ruins, and the surrounding landscape was scarred," Davidson wrote of the experience. Most important, the Union did not break through the Confederate line here, cowed by the close-range cannon fire and the impenetrable depth and breadth of the defenses assembled against them.

When you're ready, return to your vehicle on the same path and continue down the road to the next tour stop.

Take the trail from Lee Drive and walk to this field, where Bernard's Cabins stood.

Tour Stop 11: Union Breakthrough

A Daring Crossing, Quickly Foiled

(Note: This is the park's tour stop 5.)

On December 12, Union Major General Franklin and his officers spotted a weak link in the Confederate line at this wet, mucky terrain near Prospect Hill. Major General Jackson, who held the right end of the Confederate line, had not staffed this section of the high ground very heavily, thinking the swampy ground impassable and unlikely to be attacked. The veritable swamp would be tough to traverse, but its lack of adequate protection made it the logical target for the Union, striking the Confederates at their only thin spot and penetrating their defenses.

The terrain changes to mucky wetland as you approach the Union Breakthrough.

Earlier, we learned about the confusing nature of Burnside's orders to Franklin, impelling him to "seize" the Confederate right flank at Prospect Hill, taking care to keep it well supplied and its lines of retreat open." "Seize," in Civil War battle parlance, did not mean to conquer a well-defended position—orders usually said to "carry" such a position, or to seize an undefended post. As the Confederates' right flank was very well defended, Franklin concluded that Burnside did not mean for him to carry it, but to conduct an armed reconnaissance to keep the retreat to the pontoon bridges open.

As the orders came much later than Franklin had expected—not arriving until 7:30 that morning—the general did not return to Burnside to clarify his orders; instead, he chose to interpret them to the best of his abilities without further consulting his commanding officer. It seemed like this oversight would become the lynchpin in the Union's undoing—but in fact, this was just one in a series of misunderstandings and demonstrations of questionable judgment that would bring a disastrous end to the day.

Franklin sent Major General George Meade and the 4,500 men of his Third Division of I Corps to perform the task of seizing Prospect Hill. Meade's forces formed between 9:00 and 10:00 a.m. and advanced toward a swath of trees beyond the railroad, using the woods for cover as they crept closer to the Confederate line. You can see the railroad tracks about 500 yards in front of you as you look out over the field here.

Meade's men braved the marshy terrain and made it across, taking the one Confederate

"While I deeply regret the inability of the division, after having successfully penetrated the enemy's lines, to remain and hold what had been secured, at the same time I deem their withdrawal a matter of necessity. With one brigade commander killed, another wounded, nearly half their number hors du combat, with regiments separated from brigades, and companies from regiments, and all the confusion and disorder incidental to the advance of an extended line through wood and other obstructions, assailed by a heavy fire, not only of infantry but of artillery—not only in front but on both flanks—the best troops would be justified in withdrawing without loss of honor."
—**Major General George Meade, in his report on the Battle of Fredericksburg**

brigade they encountered completely by surprise. The southern brigade scattered, and Meade's men quickly took the road at the top of the ridge. By this time, however, the Confederates were ready to resist. Fighting continued here for more than an hour, with Meade making considerable headway and almost breaching the Confederate line . . . but the element of surprise won out once again—this time for the Confederates. Jackson's men suddenly broke through the woods by the thousand with nerve-wrenching rebel yells. Not only did they startle and unnerve Meade's men, they also quickly outnumbered the Union infantry, forcing Meade to retreat.

As you drive or walk from the Union Breakthrough to Prospect Hill, stop to note the stone pyramid standing quite a distance from the road, near the railroad tracks. (There's a marker on the road, so you won't miss it.)

Meade and his men crept through this woods, surprising the Confederates.

This memorial is known as the Meade Pyramid. Built by the Confederate Memorial Literary Society, the 23-foot-high granite structure marks the point at which Meade and his men penetrated the Confederate line.

In 1897, the literary society asked the Richmond, Fredericksburg & Potomac Railroad to put up monuments along their lines at historically important sites. Dismissing the original idea of wooden signs along the tracks' right-of-way, the railroad chose instead to build unusual monuments like this one—for which the railroad transported more than seventeen tons of granite to this spot. You can see this monument from Lee Drive, but it stands on the other side of the busy railroad tracks, so approach is prohibited.

Continue down Lee Road to the next tour stop at Prospect Hill.

Watch for the Meade Pyramid as you proceed to Prospect Hill.

The Death of Maxcy Gregg

On a battlefield obscured by cannon smoke and early winter's fog and drizzle, it's no wonder that Brigadier General Maxcy Gregg mistook Meade's approaching men for Confederate pickets. That error cost him dearly, however; when he ordered his men to hold their fire as the troops approached, he and his brigade were attacked. The resulting confrontation ended for Gregg when a Union bullet pierced his spine.

Gregg had been wounded before: He was hit in the thigh at Antietam—and the same bullet passed through Gregg and killed another brigadier general, Lawrence O'Bryan Branch. A distinguished officer, Gregg had led his men to defeat Union troops at the Second Battle of Bull Run (Second Manassas), even after six Union assaults.

At Fredericksburg, however, Gregg fell and did not rise again. He died at the Thomas Yerby house, a local landowner's property, two days later.

Tour Stop 12: Prospect Hill

The Confederate Right Flank

(Note: This is the park's tour stop 6.)

For more than a mile, Major General Stonewall Jackson spread his 35,000 troops along this high ground. Here the railroad embankment served as a ready earthwork, eliminating the need to create more cover and making the Confederate line virtually impenetrable. Jackson's artillery officer, Lieutenant Colonel Reuben Lindsey Walker, positioned fourteen big guns behind this embankment, where they served the army well in stopping an advancing Union force hundreds of yards away.

Prior to the Union attack, Walker and his gunmen targeted the land below and blasted it, working to head off an assault before it started. As Meade's division moved in and fought to break

At the end of the Confederate line, Stonewall Jackson's men held Prospect Hill.

Heavy artillery helped keep the Union from breaking the line.

through the Confederate line, the Southern cavalry swooped in from the far right flank to block the attack. The Union responded with heavy artillery fire, slaughtering so many horses in the bombardment that this ground earned the nickname "Dead Horse Hill" from local residents.

Even in the face of the spirited cavalry, Union Major General John Reynolds and his men stood their ground and attacked Jackson's forces at Prospect Hill, while Major General Sumner simultaneously attacked Longstreet's corps at Marye's Heights.

Like the attack at Marye's Heights, the Prospect Hill attack failed. By day's end, the Union had no choice but to retreat without ever reaching either target. The Confederates' victory at the end of December 13, 1862, signaled the end of the Battle of Fredericksburg, though the Union did not retreat until two days later, on December 15. In the interim, Major General Burnside took the time to consider his options.

Burnside, regrouping in the evening with his generals at Phillips House, was determined to continue the frontal attacks the following day—and even to lead the attacks himself. Sumner, Hooker, and Franklin, horrified by the idea, managed to talk him out of this plan, which would have brought certain death to thousands more men, perhaps including Burnside himself.

So it was that December 14 passed with no more fighting, while wounded men lay on the field of battle under the watchful eyes of Confederate artillerymen, who continued to guard the high

On December 15, the Union troops packed up and retreated over the pontoon bridges.

ground against potential attack. Only the strongest of the wounded managed to leave the field, some making their way across the river to the field hospital at Chatham, and some coming back into the town—while thousands of others lay where they had fallen, waiting for someone to help them. Soldiers who were not wounded searched for their comrades in the night's shadow of December 13 and 14, working in small groups to carry those who were alive off the fields. Others looked for food and blankets they could take from dead soldiers, fighting the damp chill of night with cold comfort.

Finally, on the morning of December 15, Burnside gave the order for his troops to move back across the Rappahannock and out of Fredericksburg. "As the day broke," he wrote in his report to general-in-chief Halleck, "our long lines of troops were seen marching to their different positions as if going on parade; not the least demoralization or disorganization existed."

The crushing defeat did not go over well in Washington, but it was worse on the banks of the Rappahannock. Dissension in the ranks simmered barely below the surface, and after another botched attempt at attack (the "Mud March" of January 1863), hundreds of soldiers began to desert. Burnside's officers criticized him when they were out of earshot, with Franklin and Hooker becoming particularly vocal and pointed in their disapproval; eventually, some of this furor reached the capital. Lincoln liked Burnside personally, but he had to acknowledge that the general had lost the army's confidence. At the end of January, he replaced him as leader of the Army of the Potomac with Joseph Hooker.

"To the brave officers and soldiers who accomplished the feat of this recrossing in the face of the enemy I owe everything. For the failure in the attack I am responsible, as the extreme gallantry, courage, and endurance shown by them was never excelled, and would have carried the points, had it been possible. To the families and friends of the dead I can only offer my heartfelt sympathy, but for the wounded I can offer my earnest prayers for their comfort and final recovery. The fact that I decided to move from Warrenton onto this line rather against the opinion of the President, Secretary, and yourself, and that you have left the whole management in my hands, without giving me orders, makes me the more responsible."

—**Major General Ambrose Burnside, in his report to Major General Henry Halleck, December 17, 1862**

Newly Preserved: Slaughter Pen Farm

While the battle for Marye's Heights raged at the north end of the Confederate line, an equally massive, bloody, and deadly battle took place at the south end, below Prospect Hill. Here the Union executed its main attack on Jackson's Corps on and around Prospect Hill, a battle that would result in five men receiving the Medal of Honor for bravery . . . and thousands more losing their lives. Slaughter Pen Farm was at the heart of that battle, the scene of hand-to-hand combat between Union and Confederate armies. As many as 4,500 men lost limbs and lives on this 216-acre farm in the space of an afternoon.

Acquired by the Civil War Preservation Trust, this land was saved from development and may now become part of the National Battlefield's protected holdings.

You'll find it on the west side of Highways 2 and 17, several miles south of Fredericksburg. The land is not yet open to the public; if you'd like to visit beyond the road's edge, call the Civil War Preservation Trust at (800) 298-7878.

When you have come to the end of Lee Drive and the driving tour, turn around at Prospect Hill and drive back up Lee Drive to Lafayette Boulevard. Turn right on Lafayette and return to the Sunken Road (park at the Battlefield Visitor Center). Walk uphill on the paved road that begins at the Sunken Road, to the dirt path that leads to Marye's Heights.

Tour Stop 13: Marye's Heights and the National Cemetery

The End of the Battle

The most dramatic scenes of the battle could be seen from here, at Marye's Heights, where Major General James Longstreet watched as his artillery and his men below decimated the Army of the Potomac.

From the top of this hill at about noon on December 13, the Confederate artillery, marksmen, and three brigades of infantry could see the Union divisions running toward them from the homes and buildings of Fredericksburg. Confederate Major General Robert Ransom, Brigadier General John Rogers Cooke, and Joseph Kershaw led the brigades here, while Brigadier General Thomas Cobb's men were at the stone wall.

Longstreet watched Union activity in town from Marye's Heights.

As you can see from the heights, the stone wall is clearly visible below. Confederate marksmen from Georgia took cover behind this wall, many escaping wounds and death behind the stone barrier's protection as the Union advanced. As the enemy got closer, Confederates from the Carolina brigades swooped down from Marye's Heights in support of the Georgians at the stone wall, bringing the total Confederate troops at the wall to 6,000. At the end of the day, 1,000 were killed or wounded—compared with more than 7,500 Union casualties.

The Washington Artillery of New Orleans began the day's bombardment from Marye's Heights, using nine big guns to tear through the Union ranks. When their ammunition ran low late in the afternoon, they began to back off from the crest of the hill, making the Union troops think for a moment that they were retreating—but minutes

From the heights, the stone wall and Sunken Road were clearly visible.

later, Colonel Edward Porter Alexander's artillery took their place. Now a fresh artillery unit rained lead down on the exhausted Union soldiers, virtually sealing the Northern troops' fate. As the sun went down and darkness came, the Union had no choice but to withdraw.

Walk along the path to the first entrance of Fredericksburg National Cemetery. In July 1865, with the war ended, the U.S. Congress authorized the establishment of this National Cemetery on Willis Hill, the site of a private family cemetery that dated back to the 1700s. George Washington's nephew, Major George W. Lewis, is buried here, as is Dr. Robert Wellford, U.S. Surgeon General during the 1794 Whiskey Rebellion.

The original Willis Hill Cemetery took a beating on December 11, 1862, as Union artillery fired its long barrage on the city. The marble gateposts stood here on that day, and they still bear the scars

More than 15,300 men are buried in Fredericksburg National Cemetery.

of that long bombardment—you'll see the cannonball crater in one, and the bullet holes in the other. The brick wall replaced the one that was destroyed during the Union artillery fire.

At the end of the battle on December 13, with no way to clear his wounded and dead from the field while Lee's forces remained entrenched in the heights, Burnside had no choice but to leave his suffering and dying men where they were. As the Union retreated across the river on December 15—taking their pontoon bridges with them—the townspeople were left to treat the most severely wounded and bury the dead. Most were buried right where they lay, in the residents' front yards or in farmers' fields. Weeks later, when Union burial parties came to retrieve their dead, they exhumed 1,973 bodies from 58 sites all over town.

As it turned out, the Battle of Fredericksburg in December 1862 was only the first of many battles that would involve beleaguered Fredericksburg and its neighboring Spotsylvania County. Eighteen months of periodic fighting would continue, and the people who lived here would learn to get along without a railroad or bridges across the river. This isolation cut off supplies not only for the Confederate army, but also for the civilians. More than once, the people of Fredericksburg gathered to bury dead soldiers after brutal battles tore through their town, and they would offer help and healing to Confederate troops who moved through after they survived battles in Wilderness, Spotsylvania, and Chancellorsville.

On May 3, 1863, the Union returned and stormed Marye's Heights once again, this time capturing it on the third charge by General John

Sedgwick's VI Corps. The Union captured eight Confederate cannons, including the two you see here on the heights. This battle is sometimes referred to as "Second Fredericksburg," but it was actually part of the Battle of Chancellorsville.

A Final Resting Place

In 1865, after the Confederate surrender, Congress created Fredericksburg National Cemetery as a final resting place for soldiers of the United States Army. More than 15,300 men are buried here, but fewer than 3,000 are identified—the soldiers whose bodies were moved here three years after the Battle of Fredericksburg could no longer be named; nor could the men who were reinterred in this ground after other battles in the area. The cemetery has its own numerical code to help you determine which are the unknown soldiers: The larger stones here bear the names of the soldiers who could be identified, while the smaller stones are numbered for the unknown soldiers. The lower number on the stone indicates how many bodies are buried in each grave.

This is the one place on the battlefield where you will find a collection of impressive granite and marble monuments, many of which honor entire regiments or divisions. For example, the large monument toward the front of the cemetery is for the Pennsylvania Volunteer Infantry, particularly Brigadier General Andrew Atkinson Humphrey's V Corps division. The tall monument at the street entrance is to the Union's V Corps, erected by their commander, Major General Daniel Butterfield.

The lower number on the headstone indicates how many unknown soldiers are buried there.

This monument remembers the Union V Corps.

In addition to thousands of Civil War veterans, about 100 veterans of World War II are buried here as well; two have their wives buried next to them. Feel free to walk anywhere in the cemetery to read the headstones and monuments. The official trail goes to the right and down the center of the cemetery.

The Confederate soldiers who died in this battle are buried in the cemetery at Spotsylvania Courthouse (also part of the National Park Service battlefield), as well as at the Fredericksburg City and Confederate Cemetery in town. You'll find it at the corner of Washington Avenue and Williams Street (more about this on page 92).

Beyond the Battlefield: Enriching Your Experience

Exploring the historic area in and around Fredericksburg can reveal insights, personal recollections, fascinating human drama, and a wealth of household names, all within just a few city blocks or a few miles of the town center. Expand your understanding of American history with visits to some of these remarkable sites.

Fredericksburg and Spotsylvania County Battlefields Memorial National Military Park, 9001 Plank Road, Spotsylvania, (540) 786-2880, www.nps.gov/frsp. Open daily 9–5. Closed Thanksgiving, Christmas and New Year's Day. Some specific sites within the park have more limited hours; check the website before traveling. Free admission, there is a nominal fee to see the film at each visitor center. This national military park tells the stories of four additional battles beyond Fredericksburg: Spotsylvania, Salem Church, Wilderness, and Chancellorsville. The park's properties include the Stonewall Jackson Shrine, where Major General Jackson died on May 10, 1863, and Elwood Farm, where Jackson's severed arm is buried in a stand-alone grave surrounded by a cornfield. Ask at the Fredericksburg Battlefield Visitor Center for maps and travel information.

From all areas of the battlefield park, St. George's Episcopal Church—which stood here during the battle—is an enduring landmark.

James Monroe Museum and Memorial Library, 908 Charles Street, (540) 654-1043, jamesmonroemuseum.umw.edu. Open Mar–Nov, M–Sa 10–5, Su 1–5; Dec–Feb M–Sa 10–4, Su 1–4. Adults $5, children $1. The only major historic site that explores

President Monroe's personal book collection resides here.

the life of our fifth president, this modest building is not a "presidential library" as such, but a vast compendium of Monroe's personal books and papers. The collection includes more than 1,600 items relating to Monroe's life, as well as more than 10,000 documents and upwards of 3,000 historic and rare books.

Mary Washington House, 1200 Charles Street, (540) 373-1569, http://www.washingtonheritage museums.org/#!mary-washington-house/cj8e. Open Mar–Oct, M–Sa 11–5, Sun 11–4; Nov–Feb, M–Sa 11–4, Su 12–4; closed Thanksgiving Day, Dec 24, 25, 31, and Jan 1. Adults $5, children 6–18 $2, ages 5 and under free. The last home of George Washington's mother, Mary Ball Washington, this house served as her comfortable residence near the conveniences of the surrounding town from 1772 to 1789. Here Mrs. Washington tended to her garden, enjoyed visits from her daughter Betty Washington Lewis, and gave her blessing to her son just before his inauguration as the first president of the United States.

George Washington's mother lived here for seventeen years.

Washington didn't sleep in this building on Ferry Farm, but he lived on this plantation.

George Washington's Ferry Farm, 268 Kings Highway, (540) 370-0732, www.kenmore.org/ff_home.html. Open Mar–Oct, M–Sa 10–5, Su 12–5; Nov–Dec M–Sa 10–4, Su 12–4; closed Jan, Feb, Easter Sunday, Thanksgiving Day, and Dec 24, 25, 31. Adults $8, students $4, ages 5 and under free; combination tickets with Kenmore Plantation $15 adults, $8 students. In 1738, Augustine Washington moved his family—including his six-year-old son, George—to this riverside farm. If young George ever actually chopped down a cherry tree and told his father the truth about it, this was where the event took place—and the museum here

For a sense of how the wealthy lived in the 1700s, visit Kenmore Plantation.

provides insights about the likelihood of this and other stories about our first president's boyhood. Archaeologists are hard at work throughout the spring and summer here, discovering new facts about the life and times of George and his family.

Kenmore Plantation, 1201 Washington Avenue, (540) 373-3381, www.kenmore.org. Open Mar–Oct M–Sa 10–5, Su 12–5; Nov–Dec M–Sa 10–4, Su 12–4; closed Jan, Feb, Easter Sunday, Thanksgiving Day, and Dec 24, 25, 31. Adults $10, students $5, ages 5 and under free; combination ticket with Ferry Farm $15 adults, $8 students. Fielding Lewis and his wife, Betty Washington Lewis, built this Georgian-style mansion as their primary residence. At the time, this home was considered an opulent demonstration of wealth and success, with its large rooms, sculpted ceilings, and carved woodwork.

Fredericksburg Area Museum and Cultural Center, 1001 Princess Anne Street, (540) 371-3037, www.famcc.org. Open year-round Tu–Sa 10–5, closed Su and M; closed Thanksgiving Day, Dec 24, 25, 31, and Jan 1. Adults $7, students $2, ages 6 and under free. Permanent exhibitions at this extensive museum tell the stories of this region's growth and tenacity during the Revolutionary War, the Civil War, and World Wars I and II. Using items from its collection of more than 8,000 artifacts, the museum showcases the Masonic tradition of which George Washington was a member, the stories of women and minorities throughout the civil rights movement, and the role the Rappahannock River played in Native American life and culture.

Fredericksburg City and Confederate Cemetery, Corner of Washington Avenue and William Street, (540) 373-6122, www.nps.gov/frsp/rebcem.htm. Open daily dawn–dusk. Six Confederate generals are buried in this city cemetery: Seth Barton, Dabney Maury, Abner Perrin, Daniel Ruggles, Henry Sibley, and Carter Stevenson; as are more than 3,300 Confederate soldiers—but as in Fredericksburg National Cemetery on the national battlefield, 2,184 of these soldiers are unidentified. Union Brigadier General Daniel Davis Wheeler, a Medal of Honor winner, is buried here as well. This cemetery was created by the Ladies Memorial Association, who purchased the land in 1867 and reinterred soldiers buried all over the area in this central location.

The remains of 3,300 soldiers rest in the Confederate Cemetery.

Historic Fredericksburg: A Tourist's Guide to Exploring, Staying, and Eating

Even recreation is history in downtown Fredericksburg, a forty-block area declared a National Historic District in 1971. Walk downtown to pick up a bottle of cabernet at the Virginia Wine Experience, shop in the umpteen antique stores, or relax with a cup of coffee and an exotic pastry at Eileen's, and you'll find yourself pausing to read the historical markers that seem to pop up at every street corner. You may learn a few things about the Revolutionary War or the people who stayed and protected their homes throughout the Battle of Fredericksburg, just by lingering an extra moment on your way to drinks or dinner—and it may surprise you that your walk through downtown Fredericksburg can be both painlessly educational and deliciously fun.

Here's one of the most closely guarded secrets in Virginia: You've actually come to Fredericksburg for the food. Wonderful restaurants tempt your palate with delicacies on nearly every street in the historic district, passionately created by inspired chefs who chose this town, just a few miles from the nation's capital, to build showcases for their culinary talent. If you want to dine on haute cuisine every night of the week, you can do it in Fredericksburg without repeating a venue—and best of all, you can walk to nearly any of the finest restaurants from your hotel or bed-and-breakfast.

Perhaps it's the town ordinance against chain restaurants and big-box stores in the historic

Historic Fredericksburg features shops and restaurants in buildings nearly two centuries old.

You'll find lots of fun shopping experiences in town.

district that draws so many fine establishments, or maybe it's the zeal for preservation that brings such interesting merchants as the quirky Griffin Bookstore or the upscale and eclectic Heritage Gifts and Imports, both of which created modern retail spaces in 150-year-old buildings. Whatever the attraction, the resulting assortment of shops, restaurants, cafés, coffeehouses, historic inns, and more is enough to keep even the most casual visitor engaged for much longer than a weekend—and eager to come back for another visit.

Where to Stay in Historic Fredericksburg

If you're fortunate enough to book early and land a room at one of Fredericksburg's captivating bed-and-breakfasts or historic inns, you will be virtually guaranteed a visit with a quietly elegant touch.

Fredericksburg offers that rare blend of comfortable, attractive accommodations and genuine hospitality; in short, the innkeepers here love to entertain and look forward to providing you with a positive experience. Full, hot breakfasts each morning, home-baked treats during the day, settees and recliners where you can relax with a good book, and even high-speed wireless Internet are all amenities at the area's most interesting lodging choices.

If you'd rather rack up the frequent traveler points at your favorite hotel chain, Fredericksburg does have its strip of national name brands on Plank Road and Jefferson Davis Highway, well outside of the historic district. You will find Best Western, Quality Inn, Holiday Inn, Super 8, EconoLodge, Ramada, Travelodge, Wingate, Hilton Garden Inn, Motel 6, and Comfort Inn on the Plank Road strip. In downtown Fredericksburg, there's a Marriott Courtyard that blends in suitably with its historic surroundings.

Home-baked goodies abound in historic bed-and-breakfast inns.

Here are some of the unique options you'll find in town:

Inn at the Olde Silk Mill (former Fredericksburg Colonial Inn), 1707 Princess Anne Street, (540) 371-5666, www.innattheoldesilkmill.com. Locally owned, this early 20th century building enjoyed an extensive renovation in 2007, turning its 27 rooms into charming accommodations, each with unique antique furnishings, high Victorian-style beds, new rugs and silk drapes, and polished hardwood floors. The boutique hotel is walking distance from most of the town's historic sites, and you'll find a custom copper art shop and other conveniences in the adjacent former silk mill building.

The Kenmore Inn, 1200 Princess Anne Street, (540) 371-7622, www.kenmoreinn.com. Restaurant open Tu–W 5:30–9:30, Th–Sa 5:30–10:30, Su 5–8, closed Mon, bar open daily 5:30–12:20. This historic bed-and-breakfast-style inn offers

At the Kenmore Inn, guests enjoy a wonderful restaurant and plenty of amenities.

nine individually decorated rooms, all with private baths, flat-screen televisions, and wireless Internet service—as well as four-poster beds and period furnishings. Ultramodern private baths make this inn a careful blend of tradition and the amenities its guests find most appealing. You'll find cream sherry and bottled water awaiting you in your room, and if you've chosen one of the larger luxury rooms, a wood-burning fireplace may be waiting as well. Enjoy a breakfast bar of pastries and coffee when you arise, and join the other guests for made-to-order breakfast entrées. Be sure to dine in the pub and restaurant on the first floor, where you'll find everything from crab cakes to pork steak with mascarpone risotto.

Richard Johnston Inn Bed & Breakfast, 711 Caroline Street, (540) 899-7606, (877) 577-0770, www.therichardjohnstoninn.com. Built in 1770 and the former home of the mayor of Fredericksburg in the 1800s, this inn feels more like a home than

Period style and furnishings are a hallmark of the Richard Johnston Inn.

even a bed-and-breakfast. The courtyard suites are modern with traditional touches, and easily as large as a New York City apartment—so you would have no idea that these rooms once served as slave quarters. A spacious dining room accommodates guests during the extended continental breakfast on weekdays, and for the full weekend breakfast (think bacon-cheddar quiche and apple croissants). Book early to be sure to get one of the seven rooms or two suites.

Where to Eat in Historic Fredericksburg

Battlefield Restaurant, 1018 Lafayette Bouelvard, (540) 373-9661. Breakfast and lunch daily. Open M–F 6–4, Sa–Su 6–2. Come here for the whopping breakfast—including some of the best corned beef hash we've ever had—just before you begin your tour of the national battlefield park across the street. The servers call you "honey," it's still legal to smoke in here (and why is that, exactly?), and the dining room fills up by seven in the morning, but the hearty, old-fashioned breakfast can't be beat for its ability to satisfy—especially for the rock-bottom price. Cash only!

The Bavarian Chef, 200 Lafayette Boulevard, (540) 656-2101, www.thebavarianchef.com/fredericksburg.html. Tu–Su 11:30–9, closed M. Owned and operated by the Thalwitz family, who have run The Bavarian Chef in Madison, Va., since 1974, this authentically German establishment features a range of traditional dishes including kasseler rippchen, schnitzel, sahnegoulasch and sauerbraten—and the reviews rave about the old-world flavors.

Bistro Bethem, 309 William Street, (540) 371-9999, www.bistrobethem.com. Open T–Sa 11:30–2:30 and 5–10, Su 11:30–2:30 (brunch) and 5–9; closed M. For our money, this is the best restaurant in Fredericksburg. Check the chalkboard for wildly imaginative specials based on the freshest seasonal ingredients available. The entire menu changes daily, so you may find quail stuffed with savory cornbread, apples, and pancetta; or veal sweetbreads; or fire-roasted duck breast; or spring rockfish with a white truffle caper aioli . . .

Brilliant cuisine and excellent service make Bistro Bethem one of Fredericksburg's best.

or something else entirely. Whatever the choices, you're assured inventive blends of flavors and textures, accompanied by enthusiastic service that crackles with efficiency. Don't miss this terrific restaurant.

Café New Orleans, 216 William Street, (540) 374-0404, tastecajun.com. Open Su–Tu 11–2:30 and 5–9, W–Sa 11–9. Traditional Cajun and Creole dishes get an innovative spin here with an infusion of flavors from the Low Country, the Caribbean, and beyond. The vegetable jambalaya is a must, and the crawfish and mussels piled on linguini with spinach, garlic, and prosciutto will satisfy your craving for fresh and flavorful seafood. Save room for the chocolate fudge crème brûlée.

Eileen's Bakery and Café, 1115 Caroline Street, (540) 372-4030, eileensbakeryandcafe.com. Tu–F 7:30–4, Sa 8–5, Su 8–4, closed M. Redefining the meaning of a quick breakfast, this innovative bakery creates a mouth-watering selection of breakfast sandwiches: Try the corned beef hash, eggs and cream cheese on crusty ciabatta, or scrambled eggs, cheddar cheese sauce, and hash browns on a buttermilk biscuit. Then top off your meal with one of the gorgeous pastries that calls to you from the display case. Lunch offerings include a list of suggested gourmet sandwiches, or choose your own from an ample menu of ingredients.

Eileen's Bakery provides artful and delicious breakfast fare.

Foode, 1006 Caroline Street, (540) 479-1370, foodeonline.com. Tu–Th 11–3 and 4:30–8, Fri 11–3 and 4:30–9, Sa 10–2:30 and 4:30–9, Su 10–2 Locally grown ingredients at their freshest go into the dishes at Foode (pronounced Foodie), which means that the simple menu can change from one day to the next to feature the best available produce, seafood and meats. Order at the counter once you have a table, and help yourself to iced tea, water or coffee as you enjoy your meal. Everything is freshly prepared to order. Don't miss the Saturday and Sunday brunch menu.

Kybecca Wine Bar & Shop, 402 William Street, (540) 373-3338, kybecca.com. Open M–Th 4–11, F–Sa 3–12, Su 2–10. Just when you think there's nothing else new for a restaurant owner to dream

Small plates and an intriguing wine list make Kybecca a hot spot.

up, this tapas bar with its Enomatic automatic wine service arrives on the scene. Purchase a prepaid card and pour yourself a sample, half a glass, or a full glass of one of 32 wines on a self-service tap—and pay by the ounce with your Kybecca card. Or order a bottle from the unusual wine list to go with your choice of nearly two dozen tapas plates: charcuterie and artisan cheese plates, macaroni and cheese with lobster and bison, blue cheese sliders (mini-cheeseburgers), or olives marinated in orange juice. You'll feel trendy just being here.

La Petite Auberge, 311 William Street, (540) 371-2727, www.lapetiteaubergefred.com. Open M–F 11:30–2:30 and 5:30–10, Sa 11:30–2:15 and 5:30–10; closed Su. Everyone in town told us to come here for dinner, and we're delighted they did. The simple but elegant menu is augmented

Don't miss the chocolate marquis cake at La Petite Auberge.

by a long list of daily specials, which has included the chef's treatment of crispy duckling or veal scallopine—two of a dozen intriguing choices. Try the stuffed mussels Auberge, which feature prosciutto and the chef's own blend of manchego, mozzarella, and cheddar cheeses (and some the server kept secret). The blackened mahimahi with bananas and spring onions is a delight. Do not miss the chocolate marquis cake, a fudgelike concoction surrounded by chantilly cream—and pair it with a glass of pinot noir for a real treat.

Sunken Well Tavern, 720 Littlepage Street, (540) 370-0911; www.sunkenwelltavern.com. Open M–F 11–9. Sa–Su 9–9. Dinner-plate-sized pancakes a full inch thick (we measured), omelets, French toast, eggs any way you want them—this is a plate piled with good food at value pricing. Lunch and

Plate-sized pancakes at the Sunken Well Tavern bring in college students and tourists every weekend.

dinner offerings include your favorite salads, sandwiches, burgers, and wraps. Located in the College Heights section of town, Sunken Well draws plenty of college students on a Sunday morning.

TruLuv's, 1101 Sophia Street, (540) 373-6500, truluvs.net. Open M–Th 11:30–9, F–Sa 11:30–9:30, Su 11:30–8. With a view overlooking the Rappahannock River and fireplaces in the dining rooms, TruLuv's offers white-cloth service and a tantalizing menu that ranges from low-country specialties to culinary innovation. Choose the grilled wild salmon with jumbo lump crab meat and citrus vinaigrette, or the stuffed chicken breasts replete with a concoction of three Italian cheeses and spinach, or a filet mignon drizzled with a cabernet reduction . . . and then stay for one of the fabulous desserts made on the premises.

Glossary

artillery: The military organization in charge of the largest weapons, including cannons. Artillery officers and their men—often called gunners—are experts in the correct and accurate discharge of these weapons, as well as the transportation of big guns to the battle site.

battalion: A military unit containing two or more companies from a parent regiment. For example, a regiment would contain ten companies (A through K), and a battalion from that regiment might contain A, C and F company.

brevet: A temporary promotion, usually authorized on the field of battle.

brigade: A military unit that is smaller than a division but equal to a regiment. Civil War brigades were commanded by a colonel, and often contained 3,000 or more soldiers.

cavalry: A unit of soldiers who fight on horseback.

corps: A large formation of troops with a common function, commanded by major generals. The U.S. Army of the Potomac had six corps organizations, each with 10,000 to 15,000 soldiers. The Confederate army's corps were larger than those of the Union army, sometimes containing 20,000 soldiers.

division: A large military unit, usually containing several regiments or brigades. Several divisions make up a corps. Training, administration, and tactical functions all took place at the division level.

flank: The extreme end of the Union's or Confederates' battle line. The Confederate army's left and right flanks were critical offensive targets for the Union, as they were perceived as the weakest points in the defensive line.

infantry: Soldiers trained to fight on foot, rather than on horseback.

pontoon: A flat-bottomed boat, used to support a structure on water (usually a bridge or platform).

regiment: A military unit commanded by a colonel, containing three battalions and a headquarters company. A regiment can range in size from a few hundred to several thousand soldiers.

rifled-bore: A gun barrel with grooves that serve to spin the bullet as it passes through, increasing its speed and accuracy.

smoothbore: A gun or cannon with no grooves inside its barrel, allowing the projectile to move independently as it passes through. Smoothbore guns are less accurate than the rifled-bore guns developed later.

Bibliography

Ayers, Edward L. *In the Presence of Mine Enemies: The Civil War in the Heart of America*. NY: W.W. Norton & Co., 2003.

Burnside, Major General Ambrose. Gen. Ambrose to Maj. Gen. H. W. Halleck, December 17, 1862. Printed as "From the Army of the Potomac: An Important Letter From Gen. Burnside," *The New York Times,* December 23, 1862. Also available online at www.civilwarhome.com/burnside.htm.

Greene, A. Wilson, et al. *Fredericksburg Battlefields: Official National Park Service Handbook*. Harpers Ferry, W. VA.: Division of Publications, National Park Service, 1999.

Hess, Earl J. *Field Armies and Fortifications in the Civil War*. Chapel Hill, N.C.: UNC Press, 2005.

Meade, Major General George G. Meade to Capt. C. Kingsburgy Jr., December 20, 1862. "Report of Maj. Gen. George G. Meade, U.S. Army, Commanding Third Division, Battle of Fredericksburg, Va., December 11–15, 1862," Shotgun's Home of the American Civil War, www.civilwarhome.com/meadefredericksburg.htm.

O'Reilly, Francis Augustin. *The Fredericksburg Campaign: Winter War on the Rappahannock*. Baton Rouge, LA.: Louisiana State University Press, 2006.

Pfanz, Donald C. *War So Terrible: A Popular History of the Battle of Fredericksburg*. Richmond, VA.: Page One History Publications, 2003.

Stackpole, Edward J. *The Fredericksburg Campaign*, 2nd ed. Mechanicsburg, PA.: Stackpole Books, 1991.

Whitman, Walt. *The Wound Dresser*: *letters written to his mother from the hospitals in Washington during the Civil War.* NY, Bodley Press, 1949.

Index

Alexander, Edward Porter, 85
Amelia Street, 48
Antietam, Battle of (Sharpsburg), 3, 4, 5, 11, 12, 16, 17

Ball, William, 26, 28
Barksdale's Mississippi Brigade, 14–15, 37, 39, 40–41, 43, 44, 50
Barksdale, William, 14–15
Barton, Clara, 35
Battlefield Restaurant, 98
Bavarian Chef, The, 98
Bernard, Arthur, 72
Bernard's Cabins, 72–73
Bistro Bethem, 99–100
Black Hawk War, 14
Bland, Elbert, 23
Braehead House, 55
Brompton, 61
Brooke, Robert, 48
Bull Run, Battle of (Manassas), 3, 11, 12, 15, 17, 18
Burnside, Ambrose, 3, 4, 5, 6–8, 10, 11–12, 13, 14, 19–30, 33, 38, 41, 46, 47, 51–53, 55–63, 65, 68, 75, 80, 81, 86

Café New Orleans, 100
Caroline Street, 39, 40, 44–45
casualties, 7, 44, 58–59, 69, 84
Catlett's Station, 18
Cemetery Hill, 8

Central Rappahannock Regional Library, 39, 40–41
Chancellorsville, Battle of, 9, 31, 70, 86
Charlotte Street, 45
Chase, Salmon P., 34
Chatham Manor, 8, 30, 33–36, 80
Chickamauga and Chattanooga National Military Park, 9, 61
City Dock, 37, 40, 41, 43
Civilian Conservation Corps, 59
Civil War Preservation Trust, 82
Cobb, Thomas R. R., 15, 48, 50, 59, 83
Confederate Memorial Literary Society, 77
Cooke, John Rogers, 83
Couch, Darius, 51, 53

Davidson, Greenlee, 72–73
Davis, Jefferson, 17
Deep Run, 37, 43, 70

Ebert House, 61
89th New York, 42–43
Eileen's Bakery and Café, 93, 100
Elwood, 34, 89
etiquette, battlefield, 32

Falmouth, Va., 20, 21–22
Fauquier Street, 41
Federal Hill, 48, 59

Ferry Farm, 42, 43, 90
Foode, 101
Franklin, William, 5, 6, 10–11, 33, 46, 47, 51, 53, 56, 72, 74–75, 80, 81
Fredericksburg and Spotsylvania National Military Park, 9, 31, 54, 89
Fredericksburg Baptist Church, 36
Fredericksburg Canal, 52, 56
Fredericksburg City and Confederate Cemetery, 88, 92
Fredericksburg City Hall, 36
Fredericksburg Ladies Memorial Association, 9
Fredericksburg Museum, 48, 49, 91–92
Fredericksburg National Cemetery, 9, 32, 39 (caption), 85, 87–88

Gaines Mill, Battle of, 13
Gettysburg, Battle of, 13, 70
grand divisions, 21
Grant's headquarters, 34
Gregg, Maxcy, 77
Griffin Bookstore, 94
Griffin, Richard, 15

Halleck, Henry, 4, 10, 19, 20, 24, 81
Hamilton's Crossing, 7, 18, 28, 44, 51, 53
Hanover Street, 15, 45, 46–48, 59
Hawke Street, 39, 40
Heritage Gifts and Imports, 94
Hewitt, Katherine May, 13

Hooker, Joseph, 5, 6, 8, 10, 11–12, 33, 70, 80, 81
Howison Hill, 28, 50, 62, 68–71
Hunt, Henry, 12, 38

Inn at the Olde Silk Mill, 96
Innis House, 60

Jackson Street, 45
Jackson, Thomas "Stonewall", 2, 4, 7, 8, 15–16, 20, 24, 27–28, 29, 44, 50, 53, 65, 71, 72, 74, 78, 82, 89
Johnston, Joseph E., 2
Jones, James Earl, 31

Kenmore Inn, 96–97
Kenmore Plantation, 91
Kershaw, Joseph, 23, 60, 83
Kirkland, Richard (monument), 60
Kybecca Wine Bar & Shop, 101–102

La Petite Auberge, 102–103
Lacy, Betty, 34
Lacy, J. Horace, 33
Lafayette Boulevard, 54, 63, 81
Lansdowne Valley, 71
Law, Evander, 71
Lee Drive, 63, 70, 81
Lee, Robert E., 2, 3, 4, 5, 6, 7, 16, 17, 19–20, 23, 24, 26–29, 41, 44, 50, 51, 52, 55, 58, 64–66, 86
Lee's Hill, 50, 63, 64–66
Light House Board, 10, 12
Lincoln, Abraham, 2, 3, 6, 7, 10, 11, 14, 19, 20, 24, 28, 34, 81

Longstreet, James, 4, 6, 8, 17, 23, 27-28, 50, 58, 65, 66, 71, 79, 83

Malvern Hill, Battle of, 12, 14
Manassas, Battle of (Bull Run), 3, 11, 12, 15, 17, 18
Mannsfield, 47, 51, 53, 72–73
Market Square, 40, 49
Marye, John, 61
Marye's Heights, 6, 8, 9, 17, 28, 34, 50, 52, 53–54, 56, 57–58, 62, 63, 64–66, 79, 80, 81, 82, 83–87
Massaponax Creek, 7, 27, 52
McClellan, George B., 1–4, 16, 19
McDowell, Irvin, 34
McLaws, Lafayette, 23
Meade, George G., 12, 56, 75–76, 78
Meade Pyramid, 76–77
Mexican-American War, 11, 12, 13, 14
Monroe, James, Museum and Memorial Library, 89–90
Mormons, war against, 11, 12

New York Engineers, 37, 39, 44
19th Massachusetts, 39, 40–41

Owen, William, 53

Parrott rifle, 66, 69
Patrick, Marshal Marsena, 23
Pelham, John, 67
Pendleton, William N., 17–18, 65
Phillips House, 46, 52, 55, 79
Pickett, George, 70
Pioneers, 64–65

Pitt Street, 39, 40
pontoon bridges, 6, 7, 20–21, 24, 29, 30, 37–39, 41, 42–43, 46, 50
Pope, John, 2, 3, 18
Port Royal, Va., 28
Princess Anne Street, 39, 41, 48, 49, 54
Princess Elizabeth Street, 41
Prospect Hill, 8, 47, 50, 53, 62, 63, 64, 70, 74, 77, 78–80, 81, 82

Ransom, Robert, 83
Rapidan River, 28
Rappahannock River, 1, 5–6, 7, 8, 15, 21–22, 25, 27, 30, 33, 42, 64, 81
restaurants, 93
Reynolds, John F., 13, 52, 72, 79
Richard Johnston Inn, 97–98
Richmond, Fredericksburg & Potomac Railroad, 21, 77
Richmond, Va., 1, 2, 4, 5, 6, 7, 10, 13, 18, 20, 25, 27, 50
rifled-bore cannon, 62
Rocky Lane, 41, 44

Sacking of Fredericksburg, 46–48, 50–51
St. George's Episcopal Church, 36
Scott, Winfield, 11
Sedgwick, John, 86–87
Seven Days Battles, 16
7th Michigan, 39, 40–41
Shepherdstown, Battle of, 17
sideburns, 10
siege gun, 68

Skinker's Neck, 7, 25, 28
Slaughter, Montgomery, 23
Slaughter Pen Farm, 82
Smith, William Farrar "Baldy", 70, 72
smoothbore cannon, 62
Sophia Street, 36, 37, 39, 41
South Mountain, Battle of, 12
Spotsylvania (and Courthouse), 9, 31, 86
Stafford Heights, 8, 22, 23, 29, 34, 38, 46, 66, 68
Stansbury's Hill, 8
Steamboat Landing, 37
Stephens House foundation, 60
Stephens, Martha, 60
stone wall, 6, 57, 58, 83–87
Stuart, J. E. B., 16, 18, 26, 67
Sumner, Edwin, 5, 6, 13–14, 21–22, 26, 28, 33, 34, 46, 51, 53, 56, 79
Sunken Road, 6, 32, 34, 44, 50, 53–54, 55–63, 64, 81
Sunken Well Tavern, 103–104

Taylor's Hill, 7, 50
Telegraph Hill, 8, 28, 50, 55, 58, 62, 64
Telegraph Road (Sunken Road), 50, 56, 60

Topographical Engineers, 10
TruLuv's, 104
20th Massachusetts, 39, 40–41

Union breakthrough, 74–76
Upper Pontoon Crossing, 36, 37–39, 43
Utah War, 11, 12

Virginia Artillery, 17
Virginia Wine Experience, 93

Walker, Reuben Lindsey, 78
Warrenton, Va., 19, 21, 26
Washington Artillery of New Orleans, 61–63, 84
Washington Avenue, 88
Washington, DC, 1, 7, 20
Washington, George, 42
Washington, Mary, House, 90
Where to stay in Fredericksburg, 94–98
White Oak Road, 46
Whitman, Walt, 35
Wilderness, Battle of, 9, 31, 86
William Street, 48, 54, 88
Willis Hill, 85
Woodbury, Daniel P., 21

Also available in the Historical Tours series:

Antietam
Arlington National Cemetery
Gettysburg
New Orleans
New York Immigrant Experience
Vicksburg
Washington, D.C.

About the Author

Randi Minetor has written thirty-two books for the Globe Pequot Press, including the nine-book *Passport to Your National Parks® Companion Guides* series and five titles in the National Parks Pocket Guides series, four other titles in the Historical Tours series, *Hiking Waterfalls in New York*, and *Scenic Routes and Byways New York*. She lives in Rochester, New York with her husband, photographer Nic Minetor, whose photos appear in this book.